Design and Innovation

A Critical Approach to Their Societal Implications

Dr. Niklas HENKE

Title: Design and Innovation

A Critical Approach to Their Societal Implications

ISBN: 979-8-88676-552-6

Author: Dr. Niklas HENKE

Cover image: www.pixabay.com

Publisher: Generis Publishing
Online orders: www.generis-publishing.com
Contact email: info@generis-publishing.com

"At the end of the day, this is all very strange. One only has to step back historically to become aware of the strangeness that is easily obscured in the face of the current universalization of creativity, of its fixation on a seemingly non-alternative and universal structure of the social and the self."

(Reckwitz, 2019, p. 13).[1]

---

[1] Our translation. Original text: "Im Grunde ist das alles höchst merkwürdig. Man muss nur historisch einen Schritt zurücktreten, um sich der Seltsamkeit bewusst zu werden, die angesichts der gegenwärtigen Universalisierung der Kreativität, Ihrer Festlegung auf eine scheinbar alternativlose und allgemeingültige Struktur des Sozialen und des Selbst leicht verdeckt wird." (Reckwitz, 2019, p. 13).

Preface

This book is written as a shorter and restructured version of the Ph.D. thesis "The corporality of affects according to design in innovation projects: a critical approach, analysis of practices, and perspectives," published in 2021 at the Université Grenoble Alpes, under the direction of Professor Fabienne Martin-Juchat, and in cooperation with the Grenoble based innovation agency Ixiade. The presented results and reflections are based on the data of the thesis. They consist of: semi-structured interviews with designers and innovation project owners; an online survey with designers; and participative observations as a User Interface (UI) designer. The book follows the principal argumentation of the thesis, but in a more straightforward manner. Some ideas are formulated in a more radical and maybe polarizing way, which hopefully stimulates discussions around the given topic.

Acknowledgments

I want to thank Fabienne Martin-Juchat, not only for the supervision of the underlying Ph.D. thesis but for the overall inspiration via her research approach, emphasizing the anthropological importance of the human body. The underlying thesis would not have been possible without the trust and support of Pascal Pizelle and Isabelle Fournié. Following the tremendous help received from Fabienne Martin-Juchat, Pascal Pizelle, and Isabelle Fournié, the responsibility for any remaining mistakes or inconsistencies in this book sits with me. Furthermore, I want to thank Tania Aïello; by having borne the task of correcting my French, you have not only invested countless hours, but also significantly increased the quality of the work. I thank my family for their support – my gratitude is beyond my competence to express. The list of persons I have to thank for plenty of confetti and the inspiration during the working periods is quite long, but to keep it short, I emphasize my gratitude towards Christian Lippitsch, Timo Ziegert, Thomas Sinkiewicz, Ugur and Onur Kepenek, Liron and Ida Lechtenberg, Werner Krumsiek, Sven Schaaf, Dominik Arendt, Sascha Hefner, Guylaine Guerraud-Pinet, Hadrien Thomas, Nina Perisse, Emilie Lutz, Jerôme Gautier, Héléna Bounab, Alex Benoît, Chloé Savot, Emilie Axerlande, Thomas Conte-Chenuc, and Pierre Serrey-Pochart. I am already looking forward to meeting you again.

Table of Contents

Table of Figures

Introduction

Nowadays, private, public, and professional life is marked by an omnipresence of modern technologies – a state labeled by Vorderer (2015) as "Permanently Online, Permanently Connected (POPC)". A large share of these technologies is developed through the specific implementation of particular design practices and through innovation projects: two activities that are indispensable for modern companies that wish to stay competitive. At the same time, these are phenomena that are difficult to grasp because they are subjective and emotional. Nevertheless, their impact on society is constantly growing. One only needs to look at the UX design of social media platforms and their underlying algorithms to visualize the political dimension of technologies – they shape users' affects (*see chapter 1 for a definition of affects*), impact individuals' identity constructions, and reorganize communication.

The design and innovation sector represents a key force in Western economies, and a necessity for socio-economic actors to engage with to remain competitive (Rammert et al., 2018; Kotler, Karajaya & Setiawan, 2021). The potential for design to access the ontological, pragmatic, and prescriptive dimensions of communication is relevant for project owners to improve the acceptability of their innovations. At the same time, design practices contain socio-psychological and epistemological features and pose managerial challenges around creativity and innovativeness (Gentes, 2017). In other words: design is recognized for its communicational potential, but remains a challenge to formalize.

To address this difficulty, design methods are becoming increasingly popular, notably through the popular technique of Design Thinking. Such methods aim to integrate design effectively into industrial contexts by structuring workflows, and by organizing the collaboration of participants. For implementation in industrial contexts, design processes have become highly rationalized. However, the actual practices of designers often seem to be out of step with those industrial contexts. Consequently, design as a discipline can be located in a field of tension between artistic expressions and their industrial applications.

Design's industrial potential for innovation project owners is linked to its ability to access the affective dimension of communication. Affects are receiving more attention in the development of new products and services since the user-centered turn (Norman, 2013/1988; 2004). In order to understand affective mechanisms, understanding the role of the human body as a constituting element is crucial (Niedenthal, 2007).

Innovation – the development of new products and services or the improvement of existing ones – is a fundamental feature of capitalism, and the source of socio-political ambiguities (Schumpeter, 2008/1942). Innovations impact private, public, and professional life. In particular, recent ones in the Information and Communication Technology (ICT) sector became an omnipresent phenomenon penetrating all spheres of society. Meanwhile, innovation is not limited to the technological field; indeed, approaches to responsible, ecological, and social innovation constantly gain more societal impact. Nevertheless, the technological domain remains the innovation sphere that impacts society like no other. The ranking of the most innovative companies illustrates this, as the top ten companies are digital ICT players (Apple, Alphabet, Amazon, Microsoft, Samsung, Huawei, Alibaba, IBM, Sony, and Facebook) (Ringel et al., 2020). In addition, the next-ranked companies (such as Tesla in eleventh place, with its main activity in the automotive industry) exhibit strong impregnation of technological innovations – especially digital ICT and Artificial Intelligence (AI).

To investigate the relationship between design, innovation, and their societal context, I will start by questioning how the link between a stimulus (a design or an innovation), an affective experience, and the human body can be conceptualized. This leads to the question: what are the roles of affects and the human body in design practices? Then: how do these design practices fit into innovation projects? And finally: what is the societal role of these design practices and innovation projects?

These questions guide the four chapters of this book:

1. Affects. I will sketch out the so-called Embodiment approach, which posits that cognitive and affective processes are grounded in the human body.

2. Design. I will dig into some of the influencing variables for the daily working practices of designers – in particular, the role of affects, methods, and of the industrial context.

3. Innovation. I will attempt to locate these design practices in the context of innovation projects, and present some of the essential mechanisms of the innovation sector.

4. Society. Finally, I will situate these same design practices and innovation projects in the broader context of society. While doing so, I will be guided by the theoretical framework proposed by the Frankfurt School, but I aim to complement their approach with the even more radical perspective of Friedrich Nietzsche, as well as more contemporary thinkers such as Hartmut Rosa and Byung-Chul Han.

In summarizing, I will endeavor to explain: how design, innovation, and technology are related; what role affects (and therefore the human body) play; and how these affects can be situated in the broader context of modern societies. With respect to their mounting socio-economic importance, I will try to do so in a critical manner, thereby hoping to stimulate the political discussion around design, innovation, and technology.

AFFECTS – or psycho-somatic-affective interweaving

The way in which affects are communicated is a key element in understanding society, and an essential element for an anthropology of modernity (Martin-Juchat, 2008b; 2013; 2020). Affects impact cognitive processes such as attention, concentration, learning, memory, and creativity, and consequently also social interaction and communication. They form a sort of permanent baseline to human existence, as they impact social capital (Illouz, 2006, p. 82), professional success (Hochschild, 2012/1983; Lépine, 2015), and perceived quality of life (Ekman, 2014, p. 8). Therefore, it may not seem surprising that they are also identified as a key factor for the acceptability of design and innovation.

The notion of *affects* encompasses *feelings, emotions,* and *moods.* Affects can be differentiated according to their temporality into micro-expressions, emotions, moods, and character traits (Ekman, 2014). [2] They can be differentiated according to their positive or negative valence and form complex, ambiguous, and/or ambivalent combinations. Affects are a matter of personal experience, depending on education and societal context, and they represent real-time indicators of an individual's wellbeing (Damasio, 2018, p. 46). In short, they provide continuous feedback on health and identity.

In order to analyze affect, it is helpful to distinguish between different levels: **1) the biopsychological level** (physiological, perceptual, cognitive processes); **2) the interpersonal level** (social interactions, communication); and **3) the group analysis level** (families, work groups, etc.) (Tcherkassof, 2008). Furthermore, affects can be characterized by "exteroceptive (tactile, odorous, thermal), proprioceptive (tension of muscles, ligaments, tendons, etc.) and interoceptive (intestinal tension, stomach acid, headaches, etc.)" sub-dimensions (Martin-Juchat, 2002, p. 9). They can be schematized as a complex set of physical and mental changes in response to a perceived meaningful situation. The stimulus can be external (for example, a novel interface, a trusted friend, or

---

[2] Microexpressions occur over a period of about fifty seconds, emotions occur over seconds to several minutes, moods can be externalised over hours to two days, and character traits last for years, life episodes, or even a lifetime (Ekman, 2014).

a wild bear) or internal (for example, a memory or an idea). The focus on the individual evaluation of a stimulus as meaningful leads to the so-called *appraisal* theories (Frijda, 1986; Scherer, 1998; 2005), which interpret affects as *relevance detecto*rs. They are indicators of moments perceived as notable by an individual; something unexpected has happened. or something expected has not happened. Thus, for design and innovation actors, affects are a gateway to the user's subjective experience.

The various conceptualizations between a stimulus, affective experience, and bodily reaction

In everyday life, it is quite easy to observe a link between affective experiences and bodily reactions – for example, changes in heart rate, increased breathing, or increased sweating linked to an affective experience and a stimulus. For the purpose of this book's focus, such a stimulus might be a design or an innovation. There are several approaches to conceptualize this link more precisely. The role ascribed to the human body changes according to these various theories, and there is heterogeneity in its functioning principles: are bodily reactions the *result* or the *origin* of affects? Are they evoked in parallel? Are they *in*dependent or *inter*dependent?

These questions divide the different approaches, which I briefly present here in order to distinguish them from the so-called Embodiment approach. Figure 1 shows different historical schemes for conceptualizing the interaction between a stimulus, affective experiences, and bodily reactions. They consider different elements and represent different mechanisms.

Figure 1. The various conceptualizations between stimulus, affective experience, and bodily reaction

A. James´ Theory (1950/1890)

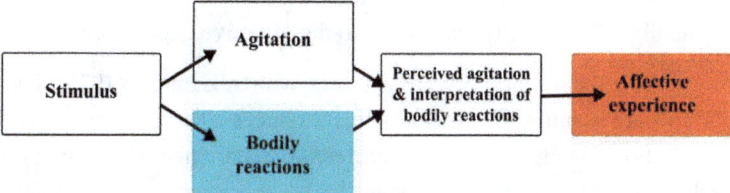

B. Cannon´s Theory (1929)

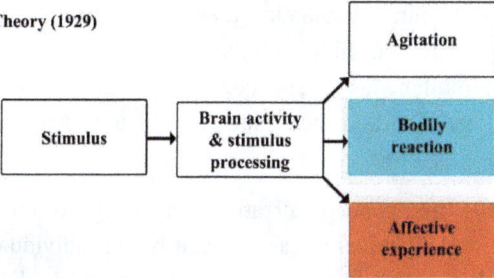

C. Cognitive evaluation theory (Schachter, 1964)

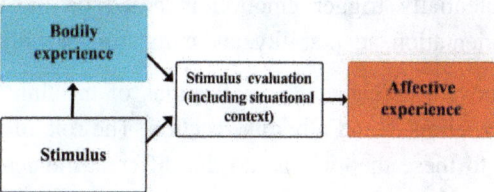

D. Appraisal theory (Scherer, 2005)

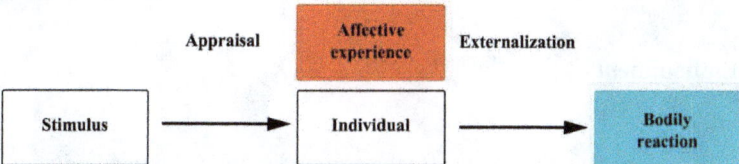

Figure adapted from diagrams proposed by Gerrig & Zimbardo (2008, p. 461) for theories A – C, and by Scherer (1998, p. 1) for theory D.

The theory of William James (1950/1890, Theory A) and Carl Lange states that a stimulus causes a bodily reaction together with agitation, which leads to the perception of this agitation and the observation of the bodily reaction, which then generates the affective experience. In this case, the evaluation of the bodily state leads to the affective experience.

The theory of Philip Bard and Walter Cannon (1929, Theory B) and Philip Bard assumes that the stimulus produces a certain brain activity that leads to agitation, bodily reaction, and affective experience. Here, the bodily reaction and the affective experience have the same source, but do not influence each other directly.

Schachter's (1964) cognitive evaluation theory (Theory C) describes the emergence of an affect by way of a stimulus inducing both a bodily reaction and a cognitive evaluation simultaneously. The cognitive evaluation includes the evaluation of the bodily reaction and the situational context, which causes the emergence of the affective experience.

Theory D presents the conceptualization according to the so-called *appraisal* theories. A stimulus, perceived as relevant by an individual, triggers an affect that creates a bodily reaction. Thereby, Scherer (2005) differentiates between the following subsystems: cognitive, subjective, expressive, physiological, and motivational. According to Scherer, the evaluation of a stimulus that could potentially trigger emotion is based on the criteria of novelty, valence, goal orientation, adaptability, and compatibility with norms.

These theories show different conceptualizations of the link between a stimulus, an affective experience, and a bodily reaction. The role of the human body differs according to these theories, as do the different elements that are considered. In contrast to these theories, let me now clarify the Embodiment approach.

Embodiment

'Embodiment' understands affect as grounded in the human body and, therefore, part of *Grounded Cognition* (Barsalou, 2008). The key assumption is that the human body constitutes the mind (Leitan & Chaffey, 2014). Embodiment

18

assumes that all physiological processes have psychological effects and *vice versa*. This means that affects, body, and the cognition of an individual are to be thought of in an intertwined manner.

An essential philosophical foundation of Embodiment is the principle of phenomenology. According to Merleau-Ponty (1985/1960), human cognition cannot be understood without taking into account the body and its physical interaction with the world. Neither the mind nor the body is passive in serving the other, but rather they are connected and interdependent. Figure 2 shows my proposition of how to visualize the idea of Embodiment.

Figure 2. The idea of Embodiment

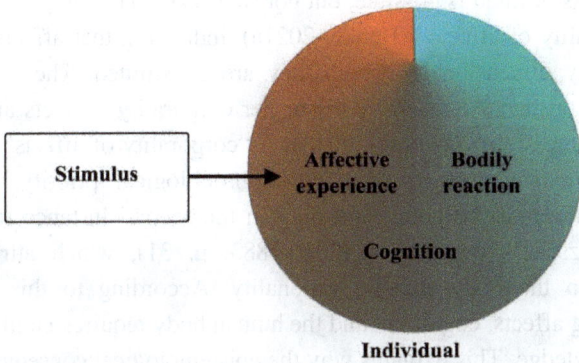

The gradient in the figure indicates co-presences of affective experience and bodily reaction. By saying *affect,* one might emphasize the left side of Figure 2, and by talking about the *body,* the focus might lie on the right side. One may focus more on one or another – hence the gradient becomes sharper at the upper end of the figure.

The differentiation of these elements has been embedded in Western thought since René Descartes' Cartesian dualism, which established a strict separation between body (*res extensa*) and mind (*res cogitans*). Embodiment rejects such a separation. Similarly, Martin-Juchat (2008b) proposes the term "affective body" to signify the unity between affects and the human body. I use the term "psycho-somatic-affective" (Henke, 2021a) to indicate the intertwining of these dimensions (psychic, corporal, and affective).

More precisely, I distinguish between a moderate and a radical Embodiment perspective. Moderate Embodiment assumes cognition is rooted in the human body without necessarily attributing greater importance to the body. In this case, affects and the human body are understood as influencing each other in a more-or-less equal way. The radical Embodiment, on the other hand, also understands cognition and affect as rooted in the body, but it goes further: indeed, it attributes *more* importance to the human body than to affects and cognition. The human body is regarded as constituting the others, and therefore as more important.

In this book, I follow a radical Embodiment perspective, mainly because without the human body, there is neither affect nor cognition. A human body without affects or mind is possible, but not *vice versa*. Therefore, one may speak of a "corporality of affects" (Henke, 2021a), indicating that affects necessarily have a bodily dimension by which they are constituted. The identity of an individual is primarily formed by his or her corporality. Affects and cognition are bodily expressions (Damasio, 2018). A "corporality of affects" implies that the human body represents the first anthropological priority: that human existence is foremost corporal, and only in the second instance rational. This follows Nietzsche's perspective (2019/1883, p. 31), which attributes more importance to the body than to rationality. According to this perspective, understanding affects, cognition, and the human body requires bodily rather than rational knowledge. This explains why the epistemological consequence of such a radical Embodiment perspective is the favoring of non-positivist approaches.

As the last point in this chapter, I wish to emphasize the social dimension inherent to the human body. An individual does not exist separately from others, but in relation to them. The relationship between an individual and his or her human body is constituted by their respective society (Mauss, 1934), and this social dimension of the body is constantly present (Le Breton, 2015/1990; Rimé, 2005). As an example, you might think of cultural dining habits or sports practices. This psycho-social reality is grounded in the physical reality of the human body in relation to other individuals and objects in a very hands-on manner.

Thinking about the importance of the physical interaction between an individual and their environment leads us to the design and innovation sector, since from these come industrial activities that shape our environment and our everyday-life objects. Recently, the mounting importance of ICT in everyday life has led to a growing importance of User Experience (UX) and User Interface (UI) design. Therefore, I will now turn towards the role of affects in the interaction with innovation, taking the following examples.

Examples of the psycho-somatic-affective impacts of UX-design

To visualize the relationship between ICT innovations and the user, let us take a brief look at the smartphone as a device, Social Networking Sites (SNS) as applications, and Read Receipts as a specific UX feature. The smartphone represents a flagship innovation that has revolutionized information and communication practices since the introduction of the first iPhone in 2007. The power of the smartphone lies in its info-communicational plasticity, expressed in the diversity of its applications. It is a gateway to the Internet and various info-communicational offerings (Klimmt et al., 2018, p. 7) and represents a modern Swiss Army knife (Miller, 2012), usage of which may be ambiguous (Vorderer, Kroemer & Schneider, 2016, p. 702). For example, smartphone usage can be perceived as stressful, while at the same time having relaxing effects (Martin-Juchat, Pierre & Dumas, 2015). The authors also show how SNS are supposed to *fight* boredom, but paradoxically also *create more* boredom. This phenomenon has become known as the Affective Forecasting Error, meaning that users assume they will feel better by using SNS, but actually feel worse afterward (Sagioglou & Greitemeyer, 2014).

Let us turn towards SNS as smartphone applications. We have seen that subtle changes in the sorting algorithm behind a News Feed can influence users' affects, as revealed in the study by Kramer, Guillory & Hancock (2014). The authors manipulated the News Feed of 689,003 Facebook users: the news shown to group A contained more positively connoted words than the news shown to group B. Subsequently, users in group A subsequently posted more positively connoted news afterwards, and group B more negatively. The results indicate affective contagion via SNS, and that the algorithms involved can significantly impact users' affects. (NB: This study was highly controversial, as the users were not informed of their inclusion in this massive-scale study of 689,003 Facebook users.)

One powerful example illustrating the impact of UX-design modifications on the user, their communicative behavior, and their affects is the so-called 'Read Receipts' or 'Seen' function: a visual attestation of having received and read a message in the form of ticks or similar symbols beneath a message (see, for example, WhatsApp or Facebook Messenger). The introduction of this principle in messaging services has had a noticeable effect on users' communication behavior. Users tend to respond faster when Read Receipts are enabled (Vorderer, Kroemer & Schneider, 2016, p. 701), and they read messages more often in a push notification window to avoid activating the Read Receipt (Mai, Freudenthaler, Schneider, & Vorderer, 2015).

Such UX-design modifications aim to intensify the connection between the application and the user. They are carried out in the economic interests of the developer, which represents a crucial point for our topic as it visualizes the link between mercantile interests and the user's communication and affects. There is a growing research body concerning the link between innovations, ICT, SNS, single UX features, and pathologies. But more important to us than the link between isolated variables is the overall trend that the introduction of technologies comes with socio-psychological and affective ambiguities. The examples described above briefly highlight the potential impact of design modifications on users' affects.

Conclusion

The affective and bodily dimensions of communication are key elements for understanding human interaction (Lépine, Martin-Juchat & Ménissier, 2018; Martin-Juchat, 2020), as well as for design practices and innovation projects. Historically, theories conceptualized the link between a stimulus, affective experiences, and bodily reactions in various ways. Using these theories as a contrast, the idea of the Embodiment approach has now also been presented here, positing that affective and cognitive processes are grounded in the human body. Put simply: without the human body, there is no perception, no affect, no cognition, no mind, no communication, and no consciousness. When looking at design practices and innovation projects in the next chapters, bear in mind that the human body constitutes cognition, and therefore creativity. Equally, a user's perception of an innovation is constituted by his/her human body.

DESIGN – as semiotic concretizations

The word *Design* originally appeared in the 15th century (Redström, 2013). However, the emergence of design as a widespread profession is more recent, as it is linked to the progress of modernity and its new info-communicational environment. During the 20th century, design emerged as a profession, became a teaching discipline, and finally, matured into a form of research (Petit, 2017). Regarding its role as such, a distinction must be made between research *by, on,* and *for* design: design can be the *means* of research (research *by* design), the *object* of research (research *on* design), and the *purpose* of research (research *for* design) (Findeli, 2005). In this book, I conduct research *on* design practices.

Today, design penetrates all spheres of private, professional, and public life (Michaud, 2011/2003) and impacts on perceived quality of everyday life (Lévy, 2018). The socio-economic importance of information, communication, and knowledge is increasing, guided by the growth of the tertiary sector in Western economies. I hold this trend responsible for the rise of design professions because, in saturated markets, design represents a potential source of communicational differentiation, competitive advantage, added value, and, consequently, economic benefits. The saturation of markets has increased competition and the pressure to improve synchronization between user and innovation – in other words: to develop products that are best suited for the affective and corporal disposition of the concerned target group. To gain a competitive advantage by intensifying the link between users and innovations, actors have tried to identify opportunities to communicate more effectively with users, and design has been identified as having such potential.

The saturation of markets, especially from the 19th Century onwards, led to an increase in the socio-economic importance of design (Vial, 2020/2015). During the first part of this period, advertising disciplines developed in parallel. Communication, design, and advertising professions gain importance through the need to differentiate communication, products, and brands since they are capable of creating affective meaning for users. The central point in product development therefore shifted from focusing on pure functionality to a more hedonic dimension (Norman, 2013/1988). The UX paradigm turned from technology-centered to user-centered, and then finally to interaction-centered product development processes.

The growing importance of design professions is linked to the democratization of ICT, which can be visualized with the following example. Before the personal computer became a mass tool, it was only usable by experts, as the mode of interaction was textual and coded. A change that promoted the computer as an innovation was the transition from textual to graphical interaction (Dourish, 2001). Once users were able to interact via a graphical interface, less expertise was required, and the computer became more accessible to many users (at the same time, production costs fell). This evolution has a crucial consequence for our topic, because the transition from text to graphic interaction was a driving force in the advancement of UX-, UI design, and graphic design. Finally, in the 1980^s, design became "hyper-commercialized" (Dunne & Raby, 2013, p. 6) and gained more weight in the development of new products and services. Nowadays, added value is more and more often found in design, helping products to stand out in saturated markets.

Defining design may seem rather difficult, as it applies to a variety of disciplines such as fashion, music, or advertising. Firstly, I present broad definitions and then converge toward a more precise one. Broadly speaking, design represents a semiotic process (Zacklad, 2019), and it is closely linked to the socio-technical, cultural, and economic spheres (Quinton, 2002, p. 17). The English word *design* can, on the one hand, indicate planning and organizational processes and, on the other hand, mean the process of giving shape to something, which is not necessarily limited to the visual sense. If considering design as the act of creating artifacts, the Caves of Gascony or flint are a sort of design. Similarly, if defining design as the act of changing a present state into a preferred state (Simon, 1971), then engineering or business management also represents a form of design. Thus, the term *design* can be understood extremely broadly.

In the following section, I turn toward a more precise definition of design. First of all, among the different definitions of design is an indispensable characteristic: the notion of improvement. The main intention of design is to change a present state into an improved future state. An elementary principle of this optimistic orientation towards the future is the distinction between a possible, plausible, probable, and preferable future, as proposed by Dunne & Raby (2013, p. 5), as well as by Redström (2017, p. 127) – see Figure 3, below. A major characteristic of design and innovation is that they try to differentiate between these possible, plausible, and probable futures and, finally, try to propose a preferable one.

Figure 3. The possible, plausible, probable, and preferable future, according to Dunne & Raby (2013)

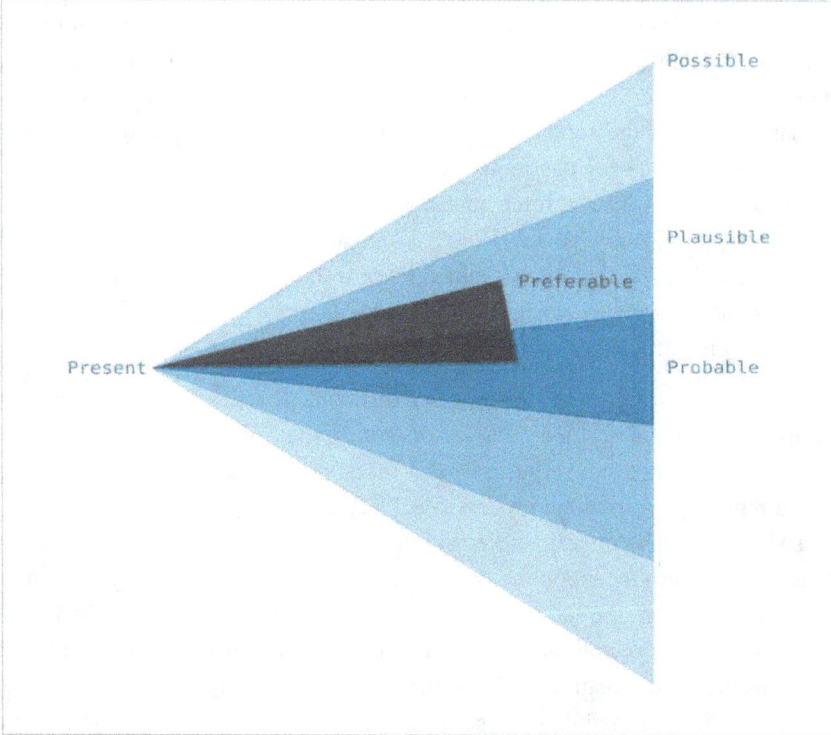

The distinction between a possible, plausible, probable, and preferable future is a key distinction for design practices and innovation projects.

The conceptual differentiations I have indicated so far lead us to the categorization of design practices according to Zacklad (2017), defining design according to a three-dimensional matrix: the type of artifact (object, visual, interaction, service, space); the dimensions of the artifact (symbolic, experience, function, form); and the modalities of engagement (classical project mode, Design Thinking, participatory design, rhetorical design). This classification is presented below in Figure 4. The advantage of this approach is that it allows one to precisely define a large range of design types.

Figure 4. The three-dimensional classification of design practices (translated into English from Zacklad, 2017, p. 5)

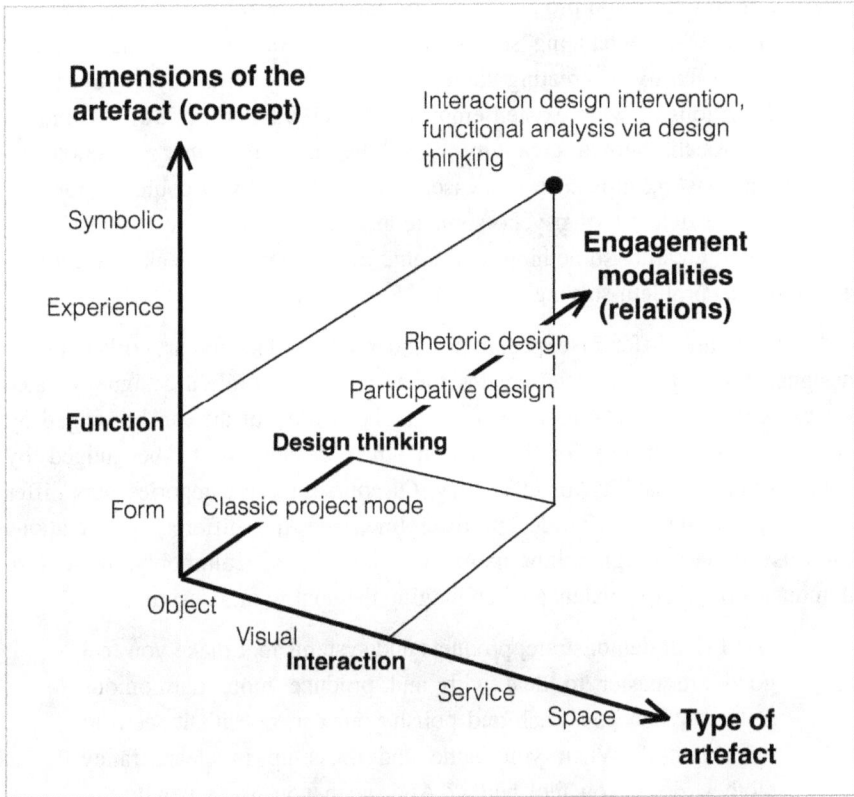

Dimensions of the artefact (concept)

Interaction design intervention, functional analysis via design thinking

Symbolic

Engagement modalities (relations)

Experience

Rhetoric design

Participative design

Function

Design thinking

Form   Classic project mode

Object

Visual

Interaction

Service

Space

Type of artefact

After having presented a more precise design definition, I wish to indicate the differences and parallels between design and art. Both mobilize creativity, and one of their conceptual challenges is defining their quality. Creativity even represents a certain paradigm in modern societies (Reckwitz, 2019), as it is part of the ubiquitous aestheticization of everyday life (Michaud, 2011/2003). Both are info-communicational, semiotic practices, which rely on mechanisms of the attention economy (Franck, 1998).

There are tendencies to attribute certain characteristics to one rather than the other. A function of art[3] may be to shock, to criticize, or to point out alternative realities – functions design can also have, but commonly to a lesser extent. For an innovation project owner, design and creativity are about creating something new or enhancing something existing. But you may have doubts about the possibility of creating something *new*. As Adorno says: "Inventions are modifications of what existed empirically."[4] (1992/1973, p. 36). According to this approach, human creativity would be limited to the restrictions of assembling existing things. In this case, increasing creativity could be done by increasing the richness of psycho-somatic-affective experiences. So, instead of talking about creating something *new,* some might prefer to speak of creativity and design as problem-solving.

There are different expectations and requirements for artwork than for designs. Put simply: an artist creates for an audience, while a designer creates for users (in a very schematizing way). If the quality of art can be judged by criteria such as beauty or fascination, then design would be judged by comprehension, usability, or efficiency. Of course, these categories may differ according to the specific design discipline, and the different expectations towards art and design might merge in some cases. Commonly, there is a dominance of positive valence when judging the quality of a design:

> "As I shall demonstrate, products and systems that make you feel good are easier to deal with and produce more harmonious results. When you wash and polish your car, doesn't it seem to drive better? When you bathe and dress up in clean, fancy clothes, don't you feel better? And when you use a wonderful, well-balanced, aesthetically pleasing garden or woodworking tool, tennis racket, or pair of skis, don't you perform better?" (Norman, 2004, p. 10).

This logic seems tempting and probably helps with many tasks and projects in design, but it is open to criticism. According to Nietzsche, the interpretation of something beautiful or aesthetic lacks the same argumentative basis as the axioms of the good or the true. The belief in the intrinsic value of

---

[3] as well as "authorial design," according to Zacklad (2017)

[4] Our translation of the original text: "Die Erfindungen sind Modifikationen von empirisch Vorhandenem." (Adorno, 1992/1973, p. 36).

the beautiful, the good, and the true is radically deconstructed by Nietzsche (2006/1886; 2008/1889), who insists that truth is neither necessarily beautiful nor good – but I will elaborate on this point later. According to Norman (2013/1988), a good product design is one that prescribes its use – that sort of *helps* the user. As an example of bad design, Norman (2013/1988) describes the so-called "Norman Doors": doors where the user does not know whether to push or pull. For Norman, this is an archetype of bad design. Currently, the leading paradigm is that design easily integrates with daily life, providing efficient apprehension and fluid usage (Norman, 2007, p. 12).

The industrialization of design

With the saturation of Western markets, the socio-economic importance of design increased, and with it, the diversity and quantity of design jobs. Today, design has become a widespread profession. This was made possible by rationalizing design and proposing methods that allow it to be integrated with industrial contexts. For operationalizing design in the industrial world exists, a variety of methods and approaches. For example, Design Thinking, Creative Problem Solving, or the Double Diamond follow similar logics. Without going into details and differences between them, these espouse: reframing the briefing, understanding user needs, ideating, agreeing on proposed ideas, and adding several feedback loops of divergence and convergence. The global intention is to integrate design effectively into industrial contexts while reducing the uncertainty linked to creativity and wicked problems.

Benjamin (2015/1936) already noted in the early 20th Century that industrial art production is increasing. Ever since, ICT innovations have changed the relationship between art, design, and consumers. Today, the means to design have become easily accessible. This trend is reinforced by the applications of Computer Aided Design. Design became a collective and complex process with diverse professions integrated. This user-centered turn has opened design to the anthropological complexity of the user and, especially, to affects – an idea popularized by Norman (2004). The interest in affects is explicitly presented in "emotional design" approaches (Walter, 2019). Today, the integration of affects is widespread (Picard, 1997; Plass & Kaplan, 2016; Walter, 2019). Norman (2004) even suggests that the affective side of design is

29

more important than the functional one. Meanwhile, a multitude of design currents has emerged, asking socio-political or philosophical questions. For Dunny & Raby (2013), design serves to express socio-economic visions and stimulate societal discourses in a critical way. Design should not only evoke positive affects:

> "One of critical design's roles is to question the limited range of emotional and psychological experiences offered through designed products. Design is assumed only to make things nice; it is as if all designers have taken an unspoken Hippocratic oath to never make anything ugly or think a negative thought. This limits and prevents designers from fully engaging with and designing for the complexities of human nature, which of course, is not always nice. Critical design can often be dark or deal with dark themes, but not just for the sake of it. Dark, complex emotions are usually ignored in design; nearly every other area of culture accepts that people are complicated, contradictory, and even neurotic, but not design. We view people as obedient and predictable users and consumers. Darkness as an antidote to naive techno-utopianism can jolt people into action." (Dunne & Raby, 2013, p. 38).

This statement questions the dominance of positive valence and shows the demand for design to participate in societal discourses in a critical way, not only by serving other professions but by taking a position of its own regarding the socio-political direction of innovations. Nowadays, design practices are heterogeneous and take different forms depending on each project, its context, and the positioning of each designer. I will briefly sum up key elements constituting design results: the characteristics of the project (including budgetary, material, and temporal constraints); the socio-psychological dynamics; the designer's imagination (constituted by his psycho-somatic-affective disposition); and their randomness (Henke, 2021a; 2021b). Some designers tend to ignore structured methods in favor of intuition and creativity. Some designers work by listening to users, while others work in a more auto-centered way. Some designers are cautious about user research, structured methods, or scientific theories – partly seen as counterproductive to creativity (Henke, 2021a). Currently, design practices are merging with other communication professions – for example, Marketing or Public Relations

(Henke & Martin-Juchat, 2021). With the democratization of design tools,[5] Design has become easily accessible to other professions, leading to a state where design is now often carried out not by designers but by other professionals – most notably, those in other communication professions.

The psycho-somatic-affective disposition of the designer

Design practices include their own ways of thinking and knowing. Intuition and abduction are at the heart of design knowledge. They often resemble an exploratory trial-and-error approach while expressing an affective, bodily, and implicit form of knowledge. Thus, the designer is in a constant but implicit dialogue between their imagination, constituted by their psycho-somatic-affective structure, and the characteristics of the project, which is done as a form of continuous "emotional screening" (Henke, 2022). What I call the *psycho-somatic-affective competence* of the designer includes the tacit dimension of human knowledge (Polanyi, 1966/2009) and refers to Gentes (2017), who presents projective abduction as the epistemological basis of design. In Figure 5, I visualize how the psycho-somatic-affective disposition of a designer is expressed in a simple stroke. Such an analysis of the creator through his semiotic expressions is commonly known in Japanese calligraphy.

Figure 5. The psycho-somatic-affective disposition expressed in a stroke

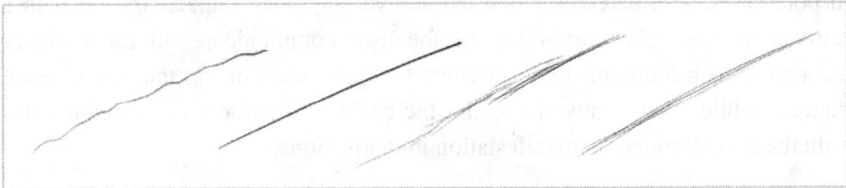

Psychological traits such as hesitation, haste, or determination become visible through such a stroke. It builds up in an illustration creating the overall mood of the designer's style. This aspect is more easily visible in hand-drawing.

---

[5] See, for example, the relatively easy access to the Adobe Creative Suite, which means unlimited possibilities for textual, audiovisual, and auditory creations.

Digital illustrations with Photoshop and a Wacom tablet often tend to curtail this aspect. The ability to curtail a psycho-somatic-affective expression, and to more easily create a line perceived as *clean,* is sometimes seen as an advantage of digital tools. Nevertheless, the psycho-somatic-affective expression remains, although it may be more abstract and may require more sensitivity to identify it. It may be expressed through the choice of photos, their assembly, the application of visual filters, or the dynamics of animations. Indeed, when transferring the example of the stroke to overall design practices, the psycho-somatic-affective inscription becomes more difficult to trace. The tool is no longer a physical brush but, for example, Adobe Photoshop. Photoshop might have a higher level of complexity than a brush, but mastering them requires a greater effort of appropriation and presents a higher degree of abstraction. Still, a design made with such software expresses the intuition, experience, and psycho-somatic-affective disposition of its creator.

Recalling the concept of Embodiment and its phenomenological foundation from the previous chapter: the human body contains a double function–expressive and perceptive. Transferring Embodiment to the activity of design implies that creation is an expression of the designer's corporality. Considering that perception is not a passive process but an active construction of meaning implies that while perceiving a design, users are in an expression of their corporality. During creation, a designer is in a feedback loop between bodily expressions and sensory perception of these expressions. The human body plays its constituting role during the creation and perception of design, and in both cases, in a perceptive and expressive way. One impacts the other in a retroactive way. The corporality of the user communicates to the designer through its consideration via user-centered approaches or via the actual usage patterns while using innovations, and the designer's corporality communicates with the users through its manifestation in innovations.

The semiotic concretization through a tacit dialogue

Design practice manifests the designer's Being in one way or another. Meanwhile, it is confronted with the constraints of the project and the interests of the involved actors. Therefore, the manifested values are to be negotiated between the involved stakeholders while trying to find a common denominator.

Consequently, a designer must exercise a certain plasticity, ensuring aesthetic and ergonomic quality. This might even define the quality of a design – a good designer is one who knows to appropriate and express aspirations that are not his own. The taste of the involved team is an influencing variable – one that is fairly subjective. The team preferences are not necessarily expressed in an explicit way, which requires sensitivity from the designer to identify them, and such sensitivity represents a psycho-somatic-effective skill. Taking these different variables into account, design practice is a dialogue between the designer's imagination and its material manifestation. The genesis of a design oscillates between these two (see Quinton, 2002). The realization of a design rarely resembles the designer's imagination perfectly, but adapts to the constraints of materials (e.g., pencils, modeling clay) or software (e.g., Adobe Creative Suite).

During this process, design allows a project to become more precise – more concrete. This happens according to a given media or while assuring the transfer between different media – for example, the transfer from text to illustration. Quite often, design practices are mobilized when a project passes from an abstract stage to a more concrete stage. Taking the example of use cases, the concept moves from a written to a visual format. Such a transition requires an appropriation of the project characteristics to specify/express them through other semiotic modalities. Consequently, I speak of design practice as semiotic concretization.

The moderation between the objectives of the project, the imagination of the designer, and the actual material manifestations requires sensitivity and plasticity in addition to creativity. According to Embodiment, such qualities are grounded in the human body. This means that design practice represents a semiotic concretization through the expression of the designer's psycho-somatic-affective disposition. I take this characteristic both as a fundamental task of design and as an indicator of a design's quality. It requires the designer to embody the different semiotic logics of the involved media. This semiotic concretization takes place in dialogue between various actors involved. The participants of this semiotic concretization are the involved team members, the tools used, and the characteristics of the project. However, when asked about the role of the body, neither the designers nor the project leaders attribute significant importance to it – over and above ergonomic aspects (Henke, 2021a). Thus, the dialogue between the mentioned variables happens largely implicitly. Summarizing, this leads us to defining design practice as semiotic concretization through a tacit dialogue between the involved actors and materialities.

Conclusion

Situating design in the user-centered turn (Akrich, 1990; Certeau, 1990; Flichy, 2003) and contemporary innovation projects, we have examined features of design professions and described underlying logics of design methods. These methods serve to integrate design effectively in industrial contexts, reduce uncertainty, ensure results, and guide the interaction between team members. Following the Embodiment approach, we have explored design practices as semiotic concretizations via a tacit dialogue between the involved psycho-somatic-affective structures, the project characteristics, and the mobilized materialities. Epistemologically speaking, design represents a form of knowledge that partly escapes rational thought.

INNOVATION – as an anthropological characteristic

The term *innovation* is often associated with radical innovations: for example, the invention of the wheel, Gutenberg's press, the discovery of gunpowder, the use of glass, the invention of telephony, the Internet, and the iPhone. However, these disruptive innovations are rare cases, and incremental innovations are much more common (Norman & Verganti, 2013). The latter can more easily be operationalized – carried out through innovation management. Given that many innovation projects fail (Stevens & Burley, 1997), economic actors try to reduce their failure rate, wherefore a multitude of factors is identified. Among them is the anthropological complexity of the user, as indicated in the first chapter.

The first stone used for a specific task by a prehistoric person might be considered a form of *technology* and *innovation*. One may see the origin of contemporary innovations and ICTs in this historical extension, even if this pathway is non-linear (Breton & Proulx, 1996; Flichy, 2003). In the meantime, technologies have become more complex, and a smartphone does not seem comparable to prehistoric tools. Nevertheless, they have a shared purpose: to master Nature and increase human powers. Initially, the word *technology* meant an individual's physiological or cognitive skills (Fuchs, 2020). However, in the 19th century, this meaning shifted to describing an application of science in the form of machines (ibid., p. 211). Technology and innovation refer to the increase of human powers: for example, a rock to hit harder, or a telescope to see further. Even the human body can be seen as a form of technology (Mauss, 1934, p. 10). The German sociologist Arnold Gehlen (2009/1940) defined technologies as prostheses of the human body, and the innovation sector intends precisely this – augmenting human powers via techno-scientific prostheses. Of note is that, through their creative wealth, humans as adaptive generalists have surpassed their initial physiological skills and produced a multitude of technological artifacts, which has led to increasing possibilities on an impressive scale. Nevertheless, this progress is linked to unintended effects: for example, ecological crises or psychosocial pathologies.

Flichy (1997/1991, p. 9) locates the origins of our current socio-technological environment between the Middle Ages and the 19th Century, but I will not go that far back, and will instead focus on more recent innovations. The contemporary socio-technological and info-communicational environment was notably forged during the 20th Century and accelerated after the 1980[s] (Miège, 2004, p. 10). Following the 17th Century, science, industry, and the economic sphere gradually form an alliance (Habermas, 1974; Mattelart, 2011), driving innovation activities. To justify these innovations, they came with promoting societal discourses and underlying ideologies. Although the innovation sector is not limited to technical innovation, techno-scientific rationality represents an elementary paradigm – the term *techno-scientific rationality* refers to the positivist epistemology that interprets Nature as a set of facts, interconnected by causalities existing independently of an observer, with a strict separation between the observer (the subject) and an object. Such an epistemology has existed for about three to four hundred years (Gasset, 1952/1942; Mattelart, 2011), but humanity has been producing innovations since the Stone Age. This means that the justifications for innovations were, for a long time, spiritual or animistic ones.

Major technological foundations that led to the digitization of data during the late 20th and early 21st Centuries were signal compression, miniaturization of components, data visualization, and algorithmics (Miège, 2015, p. 26; 2020, p. 42). Thereby, info-communicational reception via ICT has become ubiquitous and permanent – a new state of private, public, and professional life that is labelled "Permanently Online Permanently Connected (POPC)" by Vorderer (2015). As indicated, these evolutions of ICTs, particularly the intersection of computers, audio-visuals, and networks, are still reshaping Western societies (Miège, 1989, p. 16). Defining the exact beginning of modernity seems less important than the change in thinking implied by it; techno-scientific knowledge is privileged over spiritual or mythical knowledge (Ménissier, 2016).

This shift in thinking attributes more importance to the future than to the past. According to this perspective, design, and innovation, as projective improvements, gain importance. Innovation is not limited to technology or science but influences all spheres of Western societies (Rammert et al., 2018), and contemporary socio-economic actors are under coercion to innovate to remain competitive as part of fundamental capitalist mechanisms (Schumpeter, 2008/1942). The notion of innovation includes conceptual challenges because it is a tendentious term that indicates a change for the better. As indicated, similar notions are attributed to *design* and *progress*. The latter is often understood in the sense of *progress toward the better*. According to Offe (2010), innovation, design, and progress represent a modern ideology that did not exist before the 18th Century. They are not neutral, but a political issue, expressing either explicitly or implicitly an underlying value system. Therefore, they are sources of societal tensions and conflicts. Social groups benefit differently from innovations and have more or less easy access to the use and benefits of innovations. For example, those who most need innovation (e.g., precarious social groups) are sometimes the ones who have the slowest access to these innovations – a phenomenon that became known as the "Innovativeness-Needs Paradox" (Rogers, 1983/1962, p. 263). Therefore, different socio-economic actors may have opposing interpretations of innovation, design, and progress.

Rogers identified these particularities of innovation along with his innovation diffusion theory – a major approach to innovation theorization. Rogers defines the adoption cycle of innovation according to Figure 6, below. At each phase is a different social group, characterized by certain socio-demographic and socio-psychological features. These groups are "Innovators, Early Adopters, Early Majority, Late Majority, and Laggards" (Rogers, 1983/1962, p. 22, 248). The diffusion curve of innovation shows the Moore chasm (Moore, 2004), which is a crucial moment in the diffusion of an innovation. It represents a milestone at which it is decided whether an innovation will be adopted more widely or not. Considering that Early Adopters are in the phase in which the Moore chasm appears, they are a crucial target group for the success of an innovation.

Figure 6. The diffusion cycle of an innovation

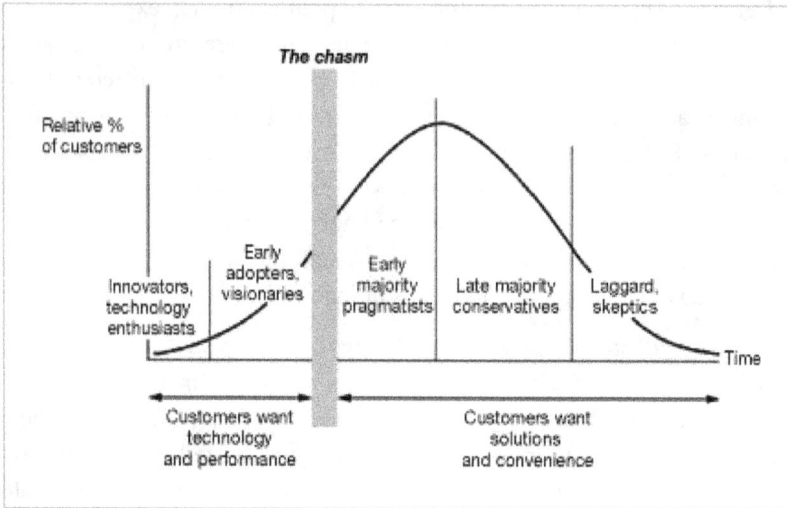

Everett Rogers' diffusion of the innovation curve, taken from Kim (2015, p. 231), shows the Moore chasm – a crucial point for the success of an innovation.

According to Rogers (1983/1962, p. 15), the diffusion of an innovation depends on its **relative advantage** (the higher the perceived advantage to the user, the faster it would be diffused), its **compatibility** (the degree to which the innovation is perceived to be in line with users' values, experiences, needs and practices), its **complexity** (is the innovation difficult to understand?), its **testability** (can the innovation experiment on a limited basis?), and its **observability** (the more visible the effects of its use are to other users, the faster it is adopted). These five characteristics of an innovation define its diffusion. The type of innovation can be categorized either as the manufacture of a new good, the realization of a new form of organization, the introduction of a new method of manufacture, the opening of a new market, or the conquest of new sources of raw materials (Schumpeter, 2008/1942). Insofar as these types of innovation take place with different intensities of disruption, a distinction can be made between incremental and radical innovation.

As already indicated, innovation became unavoidable as a stimulator of growth and a key strategy to increase productivity (Bar Am et al., 2020). This can be visualized when looking at the distribution of global spending on Research and Development (R&D). In 1960, the US accounted for 69% of global R&D spending, which dropped to 28% in 2018 (CRS, 2020, p. 1). This is due primarily to an increase in spending by other countries, notably China. Other countries have identified the importance of innovation and R&D spending to remain competitive and stimulate growth. Today, China's R&D spending is almost at the same level as that of the US. Together, these two countries are the largest investors in R&D, far ahead of Japan, Germany, Korea, France, England, Taiwan, Russia, and Italy – see Figure 7. Between 2000 and 2018 alone, global spending increased threefold, from $676 billion to $2 trillion (idem.)[6], which illustrates the importance identified in innovation.

Figure 7. The increase in R&D expenditure between 2000 and 2018 in US $

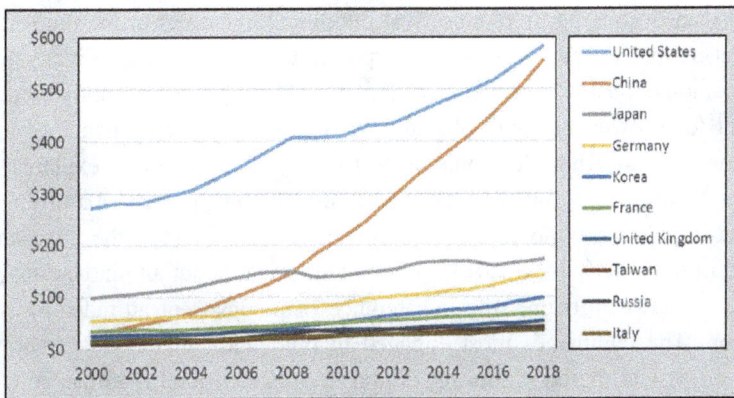

Figure from CRS (2020, p. 2), based on Organization for Economic Co-operation and Development (OECD) data: https://stats.oecd.org/Index.aspx?DataSetCode=MSTI_PUB

The geographical location most closely associated with innovation is Silicon Valley. But in terms of its current ranking on the science and technology innovativeness scale, this region is behind Tokyo, Hong Kong, Seoul, and

---

[6] Note: The figure shows the total spending and not a ranking of Innovativeness. In the Bloomberg Innovation Index, South Korea, Singapore, and Switzerland lead the ranking. Seven of the top ten countries are European, and the US actually slipped to number 11 (https://www.bloomberg.com/news/articles/2021-02-03/south-korea-leads-world-in-innovation-u-s-drops-out-of-top-10). The ranking categories were organised according to R&D activity, added manufacturing value, productivity, high-tech density, tertiary efficiency, researcher density, and patent activity.

Beijing (Dutta, Lanvin & Wunsch-Vincent, 2020, p. K-M). China (via the so-called BATX group of companies – Baidu, Alibaba, Tencent, Xiaomi) represents a growing counterweight to the dominance of the North American GAFAM (Google, Apple, Facebook, Amazon, and Microsoft). Again, the global ranking of the most innovative companies shows a dominance of digital ICT players (Ringel et al., 2020) – the ten companies considered to be the most innovative in 2020 are: Apple, Alphabet, Amazon, Microsoft, Samsung, Huawei, Alibaba, IBM, Sony, and Facebook. This top-ranked collection of four Asian and six North American companies underline the geopolitical distribution mentioned earlier. It becomes understandable, therefore, that innovation is a geopolitical issue, showing that even though innovation is not limited to technology, the two are intrinsically related.

Instead of looking more closely at the global dynamics of the innovation sector, let us turn to the national and corporate levels. The need to innovate is present among business leaders; 84% of leaders perceive innovation as important for growth, but only 6% are satisfied with the performance of their innovation efforts (Roth, Koivuniemi & Doherty, 2020), which explains the quest for factors impacting the success of innovation projects. According to Ringel et al. (2020), innovation is a top priority for 45% of the companies surveyed in their study ($N = 1,014$), 30% are skeptical about an innovation, and 25% fall in between, expressing indifference or inconsistent attitudes towards innovation. The companies most engaged in innovation in this study show a specific interest in digital platforms, digital design, Artificial Intelligence (AI), and mobile solutions (p. 5), which shows, once again, the intertwining of innovation and technology.

A company's innovativeness does not only depend on the level of R&D expenditure or the technologies available to its teams. It also requires a culture that is conducive to the emergence of creativity. According to Jaruzelski, Chwalik & Goehle (2020), the most innovative companies are characterized by the following aspects: 1) synchronization of the innovation strategy with the corporate strategy; 2) Creation of an innovation culture throughout the company; 3) Involvement of top management in the innovation programs; 4) Close contact with users; 5) Rigorous selection of projects upstream of the innovation process; and 6) Integration of these five aspects into a single customer experience. These six characteristics common to the most innovative companies show that innovation is not only a techno-scientific challenge but a socio-psychological one.

40

The innovation sector resembles the cultural industry, as they share a commonality of dealing with the difficulties of creativity, attention, info-communication, and knowledge, and they imply an inherent uncertainty about the success of their productions (Miège, 2017; 2020). It is difficult to predict which cultural productions will be successful or not and to what degree, in a similar way that it is difficult to predict the success of an innovation. Stevens & Burley (1997) note the need for 3000 raw ideas to achieve one commercial success. More precisely, 3000 raw ideas led to 300 considered ideas, 125 small projects, nine developments, four major developments, 1.7 launches, and, finally, 1 success.[7]

Figures indicating the failure rate of innovation projects are between 80% and 95%.[8] Literature on failure rate suggests that differences are correlated with the maturity of the project at which the analysis is started. According to Steven & Burley (1997, p. 7), 99.7% of submitted ideas and 40% of launched projects fail.[9] To avoid falling into the 80% - 95% of innovation projects that fail, different causes, means, and tools are identified. According to the French innovation agency Ixiade, the main causes of failure in innovation projects are: "insufficient knowledge of the user and uses, insufficient knowledge of the market, poor timing, incorrect estimation of the market value, poor consideration of the ecosystem, lack of methodology and skills, psychological bias and preconceived ideas, and a targeting error in product development" (Ixiade, 2020, p. 26).

To reduce the probability of failure, the main goal is to predict an innovation's acceptability – that is, to anticipate the behavior of potential users, their affective reactions, and their cognitive evaluations of an innovation. To address the uncertainty of innovation and design, the innovation sector encompasses a variety of research fields – marketing, engineering, management, design, sociology, psychology, linguistics, and a variety of other professions according to the needs of each project – and consequently we witness a variety of positionings of innovation agencies (Glennie & Bound, 2016, pp. 22-25).

Innovations have socio-psychological implications beyond their technical applications. For example, the invention of the washing machine did not only

---

[7] This rate varies between sectors.

[8] For example, 80% were reported by UMI (2020), and 95% were reported by Nobel (2011).

[9] Again, such a calculation depends on the definition of a project being launched.

change the way we wash clothes, but impacted the rhythms of life and affected the perception of hygiene (Trentmann, 2016, p. 4). Innovations and ICTs are not mere technological objects, but embody and express values (Habermas, 1973/1968; 1974; Miège, 2020). This includes socio-political values, spiritual beliefs, and metaphysical promises; in short: it is a vision of the relationship between human beings and the world. Simondon (2012/1958) and Habermas (1973/1968; 1974) show that technologies express the thinking inherent to their creative process. Similarly, Marcuse (1991/1964; 1969) indicates the implementation of political orientations in technologies. The most fundamental metaphysical beliefs addressed by technological developments are, according to Gasset (1952/1942, p. 38, p. 67), Simondon (2012/1958), and Mumford (2000/1952), the fear of the instability of Nature, and the augmentation of psycho-somatic-affective capacities. Techno-scientific rationality and the contemporary innovation sector feed on the metaphysical hopes of mastering Nature, decorporalization, info-communicational democratization, and systemic stabilization. Hence Ménissier (2021) speaks of innovation as a paradigm of Western societies that are supposed to give meaning to human existence and its future.

The industrial revolution, and for example, the innovations of the vacuum cleaner, the dishwasher, or the washing machine, reduced the involvement of the human body in everyday tasks (Lieberman, 2013). Modern innovations have led to a decrease in bodily activities, and in particular, ICT innovations have reinforced this process. Virilio (1990, p. 35) notes that the transition from mechanical to digital media promotes a decorporalization. Bodily activity declined, but the use of ICTs still requires bodily involvement to manipulate them. However, the way in which a touch screen is handled evokes a certain relationship with the world. Changes for the human body, brought by the introduction of new technology, are described through the example of the emergence of electricity by Virilio:

> "Accustomed to lighting a lamp or candle and carrying the torch to the table or fireplace, the technical surprise of electricity did not require concern lighting, the improvement of luminosity, but the very gesture of lighting, the bodily gestures of the person who lights and carries the light. With the control of the electronic environment, it is no longer just a question of the mutation of a familiar gesture, but this time, of behavioral ergonomics as a whole, with the exception, perhaps, of the act of feeding oneself,

washing oneself, dressing oneself or going to the toilet..."
(Virilio, 1990, p. 127).

Thus, even if the ideal of decorporalization (in the sense of liberation/emancipation from the human body) is not achieved, a change in the involvement of the human body in daily life is linked to innovations. The described value of decorporalization can be questioned in a critical manner from an Embodiment perspective, as I will do in the following sections.

The values promoting innovation and their non-fulfilment

In the 18th Century, socio-economic discourse started to emphasize that consumption not only serves individual pleasure but national prosperity through increased industrial production (Trentmann, 2016), which therefore strengthened the focus on the consumer/user. But it was not until the end of the 20th Century that the figure of the user gained significant importance (Akrich, 1990; Mallein & Toussaint, 1994). Nowadays, the contemporary innovation sector is interested in the user to reduce the failure rate of innovation projects. To this end, the user is identified as a variable to gain competitive advantages. **The value proposed by innovation agencies is twofold: to increase the chance of success of the project leaders' innovation concept; and to allow users to participate in the development of innovations that better meet their needs.**

Modern user-centered approaches transcend techno-determinist ones by including the individual (the user) and the context (the situation of use and its societal environment) (Mallein & Toussaint, 1994). The focus on the role of the user emerged alongside a paradigm of usability: in an ideal case, using products, services, or interfaces is meant to be unconscious, non-invasive, and natural (Gentes, 2017, p. 66). Innovation, and TIC developments aim to make them sort of *disappear* in everyday life – using them without being conscious about it. This paradigm of product and service design was popularized by Norman (2013/1988) but represented Heidegger's (1963/1927) differentiation between present-to-hand and ready-to-hand. The former represents the state when a tool is usable by a user, but he/she is conscious about using it, and the latter signifies the state when a user is using a tool without being conscious about using it – a usage without reflection. For example, learning to play a musical instrument represents the transition from present-to-hand to ready-to-hand. Equally, the paradigm of the user-centered turn aims to move from a present-to-hand state of innovation usage to a ready-to-hand one. Since innovations are perceived novelties, their usage starts with the present-to-hand stage (leaving aside small upgrades of existing tools); in this stage, the user rationalizes the innovation before becoming sufficiently familiar with using it unconsciously (ready-to-hand). The user-centered approach is intended to facilitate this transition.

At the beginning of the 20th Century, media research started with the behaviorist question: **what influence do media have on people?** Research aimed to explain the media mechanisms of the propaganda of that time. But, gradually, the user was no longer seen as passive, and the communication channel no longer as neutral. Lazarsfeld, Berelson & Gaudet's "Two-Step Flow of Communication" (1944) began to crack the behaviorist approaches by noting that between the distribution of a message and its reception are so-called "opinion leaders," who impact the final perception of a message. Nevertheless, during the mid-20th Century, the user/consumer was still broadly considered in a passive way, which is reflected in the long-time dominant Stimulus-Response approaches, which interpreted mass communication in a unidirectional way. As already mentioned, this view changed over time, and during the end of the 20th century, the user was considered to take an active role and individually construct meaning through everyday uses by tinkering in an autonomous, exploratory, and creative way (Certeau, 1990).

Towards the end of the 20th century, the focus turned to the user, asking: **what do people do with the media?** (Proulx, 2005). Rather than conceptualizing a passive receiver, an active one who individually constructs meaning was considered instead. This perspective was popularized by the Uses and Gratification Theory (Katz, Blumler & Gurevitch, 1974). Nowadays, approaches insist on the fact that the diffusion of innovation does not only depend on its technical performance, but on the individual construction of meaning via the user. Diffusion is impacted by the ideological, political, and cultural spheres and their respective value systems. The user is thought of in an increasingly complex way and consideration is given to affects and the human body.

Bringing us to the modern day, the above-mentioned question is asked rather reflexively in the form: **how do media and users constitute each other?** Project owners and designers try to make an innovation as suitable as possible for the respective target group. Therefore, they encounter the user via market research methods; for example, interviews, focus groups, or online studies. This helps to identify needs, adapt a concept accordingly, and in consequence, enhance the possibility of a project's success. The user-centered turn represents a shift away from a techno-determinist, unidirectional and mechanical view towards a dynamic, active consideration of the user. Therefore, it represents a remarkable socio-economic phenomenon, as it reinforces the integration of the individual in industrial processes, especially by considering the affects and the human body (Martin-Juchat & Staii, 2016). While doing so, design methods represent an operationalization of creative forces for commercial purposes. These creative forces are interesting for project owners because they can address the affective dimension of communication as in no other discipline. Therefore, they are part of what Martin-Juchat (2013) calls "the new spirit of capitalism" or "digital affective capitalism," according to Alloing & Pierre (2017, p. 11). But, paradoxically, it seems that by integrating design practices into rational logic, the project owner loses the tacit knowledge and affective potential from which the initial mercantile interest stems.

Keeping the user-centered turn in mind, let us look at the actual daily practices of designers and innovation agencies. There are quite different ways of integrating users in design practices and innovation projects. In some cases, any user research approach is rejected in the name of the creativity and ingenuity of the designer, who is taken as an archetypal user, and representative of the target group. In extreme cases, the designer supposes to know even better than the user what the user might need. At the opposing end of the spectrum are approaches based on carrying out user research via structured methods and tools, placing a high value on user feedback. In this case, user research is perceived as a competitive advantage. In yet other cases, teams show a willingness to take users into account, but they do so in an unstructured way and sometimes without meeting any users, but only by imagining fictitious ones. The preferences and opinions of the team are taken as representative values of the target users. In this case, user research could help to detect misconceptions and to test assumptions about the users. It could test the actual perceptions of a design and validate the team's visions if they are indeed in line with the target audience.

Interestingly, integrating the user in New Product Development (NPD) processes implies that the user himself carries out part of the conception, and therefore the user-centered turn represents a sort of outsourcing of R&D. The user-centered turn provides the argument that innovations are developed according to the interests of the individual – even more so by considering affects and their corporality, serving as an argument to justify the diffusion of an

45

innovation. Once developed, innovations play on users and influence their daily lives. Therefore, users and innovations have a reflexive relationship. The user impacts the development of innovation through user-centered approaches, and the innovation affects the user through its usage and its impact on daily life.

As already indicated, the initial values accompanying the emergence of ICTs after the second half of the 20th Century included freedom to access to information, horizontal distribution of political power, increased systemic stability, web-neutrality, and a sort of liberation from the human body (Miège, 2004; Cardon, 2010; Lanier, 2014; Cole & Urchs, 2015; Le Breton, 2015/1990). These values were used as arguments to justify the societal integration of innovations. They share the perception of design and innovation as improving progress (Flichy, 2003), according to which the past would be worse than the present, and the future (potentially) better. Despite these hopes placed in the emergence of innovations (and especially ICTs), unintended effects are associated with their use, which forms a paradoxical side of progress. Notwithstanding the founding values, technologies imply unintended ambiguities and ambivalences that contrast these values. For example, the idea of web neutrality, which basically means that all data is treated in the same way from its point of departure to its point of arrival, has become a difficult political issue (Cardon, 2010; 2015) because it has its limits when confronted with the mass of today's data. The quantity of data requires applying a hierarchy to each piece of information – which is done, for example, via the PageRank algorithm (Google) or EdgeRank (Facebook). Such hierarchizations are used to navigate the mass of data efficiently, but they pose justificatory problems and become a delicate political issue: how does one justify the criteria for prioritization? For the moment, a major justification was the collective intelligence paradigm: the more a website is connected, the more relevant it would be (by weighting each link according to its own relevance). But even this approach may be criticized as "The Cult of the Amateur" (Keen, 2013/2007). So, despite the technological progress initiated by innovations, and their non-negligible societal changes, should their role be relativized? Yet, the promises of modern innovations seem not fulfilled: techno-scientific progress has generally improved neither the habitability of the world (given the ecological crises) nor the psychosocial sphere (given mounting burnout rates, depression, precariousness, or an increasing rich-poor gap). At the same time, techno-scientific innovations account for undeniably positive achievements and stabilizing effects (e.g., enhancement of healthcare and social systems in certain societies). This dialectic, between the values promoting modern innovations and their non-fulfillment, can be labelled *as the inherent ambiguity of progress.*

Operationalization of design

In saturated markets, design is important to socio-economic actors for communication and promotional reasons. It conveys the potential for strategic differentiation, identity construction, and, consequently, economic advantage. It can implicitly play on the ontological, pragmatic, prescriptive, and affective dimensions of communication. These characteristics of the design are applied in the innovation sector to reduce the failure rate, to increase the acceptability of an innovation, and to improve the diffusion of an innovation. Previously I indicated how design serves the semiotic concretization of an innovation project and pointed towards the role of the psycho-somatic-affective disposition of a designer. However, this is only one variable, among others, that constitutes design processes. Other variables are the characteristics of the project, budgetary-, material-, and temporal constraints, the psychosocial dynamics of the team, and a certain randomness. All of these impact design practices and innovation projects. A designer acts in a dynamic negotiation between these components and tries to find a common denominator on which the involved actors agree. This process happens not as the result of a dematerialized mind but, as "sedimentations" (Adorno, 1992/1973, p. 15) of the materialities and psycho-somatic-affective structures involved.

The paradigm inherent to innovation projects aims to make usage ready-to-hand. In some cases, an unconscious use is certainly preferable – for example, for critical situations where the usage plays a safety role. Some designs should certainly not necessarily evoke reflexivity. However, there are others for which one may ask whether design should maybe provoke doubts or questions and participate in the socio-political discourse. This would be *Critical Design* in the sense of Critical Theory – a design that takes a socio-political stand instead of trying to be neutral (leaving aside to which degree that is possible). This view should not be confused with the *Critical Design* of Dunne & Raby (2013). Their approach shares a skeptical view of the status quo, but it is not thought of in the tradition of Critical Theory.

Exploiting design potential creates certain management challenges that appear when the practices of designers are not in phase with the logic of the methods supposed to operationalize design. Schematizing this, the methods follow functionalist logic, and the designers' practices are led by intuition, experience, and tacit knowledge. The design seems difficult to manage, but can create economic value through several notions. Design processes stimulate ideas, creativity, or inspiration. on the contrary, some design practice is done logically and causally. The constraints set by the Corporate Identity Guidelines of a company and the respective characteristics of a project might determine a large part of the design process. This part of the design can more easily be operationalized. It requires less creativity and theoretically could be done by AI, which leads to the identification of design in a field of tensions between artistic expressions and their applications in industrial contexts. Operationalizing design means managing these tensions to exploit the design's economic potential.

Operationalization of psycho-somatic-affective structures

"I feel strong emotions through consumption; therefore, I am." (Martin-Juchat, 2014, p. 8).

Affects play a major role in differentiating communication, products, and brands. The aim of integrating affects into the design and innovation process is to strengthen the product-user- and the brand-user relationship. Therefore, the operationalization of design via innovation agencies is part of a broader process of exploiting affects.[10] Via the lens of economic actors, the consideration of affects is done to rationalize affects into an industrially manageable mode. A well-known example is the Facebook Like-Button (Alloing & Pierre, 2017). The role of design is considered in this process to ensure a certain control of affects according to the objectives of the socio-economic actors. Interestingly, affects are seen as an inherent part of the design, and the design's affectivity is often taken as an indicator of its quality. However, for the majority of designers, the

---

[10] Concerning the exploitation of affects via socio-economic actors, see Illouz (2006), Hochschild (2012/1983), Martin-Juchat (2013; 2014), Martin-Juchat & Staii (2016), or Alloing & Pierre (2017).

consideration of affects via structured methods is not very present during daily practices (Henke, 2021a). Most of the time, they are considered in an implicit way. The human body is even less explicitly present. It seems surprising that affects are considered remarkable for a design, but that they are not addressed in an explicit or structured way. Therefore, the incoherences of design practices most relevant to our topic are: 1) A discrepancy in the evaluation of design quality (quality perceived as objective vs. subjective); 2) a conflict about the integration of the user (user-centered vs. self-centered practices – with graduations between them); 3) A discrepancy between communication theories and communication practices; 4) A discrepancy concerning the role of affects (affects are perceived as an important element of design, but structured approaches are rare); and 5) a disagreement on the consideration of the human body (a role is attributed to the body as an object responsible for the perception via the five senses, but approaches specifying or systematizing its role are mostly absent). The body is not perceived as a constitutive element of design practices (only rarely), which contrasts the Embodiment approach.

An essential aspect of design practices is to realize semiotic translations between different media; for example, to translate the characteristics of an innovative concept into visual representations – from text to image. During this transfer, the content becomes semiotically more concrete; hence I introduced the term semiotic concretization – equivalent to Adorno's "sedimentation" of function into form (1992/1973, p. 15). A multitude of possible links between form and function can be observed. As mentioned above, the "sedimentation" of function into form follows, according to our observations, the psychosocial dynamics of the team involved, the characteristics of the respective project, the material, budgetary and temporal constraints, and certain randomness.[11] This *magical* side of human creative forces is operationalized by innovation agencies according to functionalist rationality to finally be integrated into industrial processes. Therefore, design finds itself in tension between the artistic expressions of implicit psycho-somatic-affective knowledge and its application in an industrial context through functionalist rationalizations. Project owners operationalize design as a psycho-somatic-affective competence to impact the affective dimension of communication.

---

[11] The element of randomness in conception processes refers to a certain *creative magic*– Benjamin (2015/1936) uses the term "aura" to describe the expression of this dimension, as does Adorno (2007/1977) in his letters to Benjamin.

Conclusion

Since the failure rate of innovation projects is high, actors try to identify variables influencing an innovation's acceptability. Design, affects, and, more broadly, the anthropological complexity of a user are identified as such. The value proposition of innovation agencies is to reduce the failure rate of projects, and for doing this, the human factor is identified as essential. We have explored the key concepts of innovation: the diffusion theory, adopter categories, Moore's chasm, common reasons for innovation failures, as well as methods and tools applied in innovation projects. The increasing socio-economic importance of information, communication, and knowledge reinforce the mechanisms of the attention economy, and as a result, design is becoming increasingly important for the construction and maintenance of socio-economic identities and public relations (Taylor & Botan, 2004). The discussion presented above has shed light on the political dimension of innovations before specifying the liberal values by which innovations were promoted since the second half of the 20th Century and indicated that, so far, these values have not been realized: "The Internet is no longer the utopian space of exchange and sharing, free, gratuitous and egalitarian, of which a few pioneers dreamed. It is increasingly a reflection of our societies: a large global hypermarket open day and night, where we trade all the things our bodies and minds need (and often don't need)." (Staii, 2014, p. 146).

Today, innovation projects take a central place in the strategy of companies (Kelley, 2001; Kotler, Kartajaya & Setiawan, 2021), as does the place of design in innovation projects and the place of affects in modeling the user. In saturated and highly competitive markets, innovation and design are levers of growth and potentially a competitive advantage. Innovation projects integrate design practices in the continuation of an evolution that Poirson (2014, p. 275, referring to Lipovetsky & Serroy, 2013) describes as "After art-for-the-Gods, art-for-the-Princes, and art-for-art, it is now art-for-the-market." A synonym for "art-for-the-market" could be "design".

SOCIETY – and the ambiguity inherent to progress

For situating design practices and innovation projects in their societal context, I discuss the perspective of a so-called Critical Theory in the following sections, complemented by the reflections of Friedrich Nietzsche and contemporary critical thinkers such as the sociologist Hartmut Rosa or the philosopher Byung-Chul Han. But first, it is necessary to look at the historical context of the institution that established the approach that became known as Critical Theory, which is the Frankfurt School – officially the *Institute for Social Research* (*Institut für Sozialforschung, IfS*).

Founded in 1923 by the legacy of Felix Weil, its intention was to create an institutionalization for rethinking Marxism (Wiggershaus, 1991/1988; Jay, 2018/1973). Even though, for example, Adorno denied drawing political consequences from his analyses, one can say that the Frankfurt School's thinking is politically nuanced. Weil's intention was to create a place for the discussion of Marxist ideas outside political and institutional constraints, and the members of the institute had to be in tune with his political ideology (ibid., p. 32). Felix Weil was not a member of the Communist Party, but was active in the right-wing current of it (Wiggershaus, 1991/1988). It is rather difficult to define the Frankfurt School approach precisely, as it brings together various authors with heterogeneous positions. [12] In this book, I refer mainly to the works published between the years 1930 and 1970, which I regard as the most fundamental works of Critical Theory. Each member of the Frankfurt School shows a slightly different anthropological and epistemological positioning. Nevertheless, I will try to outline the common idea.

Frankfurt School thinkers systematized the idea that everyday life is invaded by techno-scientific rationality, which prevents living a *good life* via the loss of autonomy and freedom (the notion of a *good life* will be discussed later). The common thread of Critical Theory is Marxist, dialectical, and critical

---

[12] The most widely known authors are Adorno, Horkheimer, Benjamin, Marcuse, and Fromm in the first generation, Habermas in the second generation, and Honneth and Sutterlüty in the third generation.

thinking, and, more specifically, the interpretation of modernity as a societal pathology that prevents individuals from achieving a "good life" (Honneth, 2016/2007). A key aspect of Critical Theory is the notion of *societal pathology*. According to the authors of the Frankfurt School, modern pathologies are so totalitarian that they diagnose a "pathology of normality" (Fromm, 1991/1973; 2006/2005; Adorno, 2014/1951). Social pathology is not identified as such by the individual because it represents a societal norm. From the analyses of societal pathologies, Critical Theory aims to provide the theoretical framework for the realization of a happier and freer psychosocial life. The main cause for modern societal pathologies is identified behind capitalist mechanisms that would induce reification (*Verdinglichung*), blindness (*Verblendung*), and alienation (*Entfremdung*). Honneth & Sutterlüty – recent directors of the institute – describe the Frankfurt School perspective as follows:

> "Modern science is entirely under the aegis of the mastery of Nature and its technical usability, which pushes people away from what they have power over and deprives them of any capacity for an authentic experience. According to Horkheimer and Adorno, this applies not only to the outer Nature but also to the inner Nature of human beings. In social unrest, the inner Nature of human beings is so tainted that subjects, in order to be able to exist, deny their own drives and needs and finally carry out the renunciation of happiness and pleasure that is imposed upon them. At the same time, the narrative continues, morality and law in the bourgeois era and even more so in the post-bourgeois era degenerate into cynical instruments of domination that are only meant to morally cover economic profit and legalize the pursuit of power interests by the ruling social forces. The products of the entertainment industry and mass culture, in turn, propagate a conformist adaptation to the existing and manipulate subjects in such a way that they become fungible and uncritically integrated into the reproduction of the same old thing." (Honneth & Sutterlüty, 2011, p. 71).[13]

---

[13] Our translation. The original text: "Die moderne Wissenschaft stehe ganz unter der Ägide der Beherrschung der Natur und ihrer technischen Verwertbarkeit, was die Menschen zur Entfremdung von dem treibe, worüber sie die Macht ausüben, und sie jeglicher Fähigkeit zu authentischer Erfahrung beraube. Das betrifft nach Horkheimer und Adorno nicht nur die äußere Natur, sondern auch die innere Natur der Menschen. Diese werde im

They speak of an "inner Nature of human beings" – I would call this according to the Embodiment approach, their *psycho-somatic-affective disposition*. They also speak of "drives", which includes that which can be gathered under the term *affects*.

Inherent to the Frankfurt School approach is the critique of rationality and skepticism towards the belief in progress for the better. Previously, I indicated that design and innovation's underlying value is exactly this – realizing progress *towards the better*. This already indicates how Critical Theory questions the promoting values of design and innovation. To understand their approach more precisely and to transfer it to today's innovation sector, I will clarify their critique of rationality, and especially the negative dialectic in the following section.

The critique of techno-scientific rationality

The Frankfurt School identified techno-scientific rationality as a core driver of modern societal pathologies, stating that the techno-scientific progress of modernity promises freedom, wellbeing, and emancipation, but that these promises are not kept.[14] Instead, individuals would be alienated in several ways, and the role of Critical Theory would be to reveal these abuses to achieve a societal form that allows the individual to realize a so-called *good life*. The notion of a *good life* is a crucial point in Critical Theory. It refers to an epistemology that is normative and not neutral. Instead, science should include an ethical and ideological stance to situate research findings in the context of

---

gesellschaftlichen Getriebe so zugerichtet, dass die Subjekte, um bestehen zu können, ihre eigene Trieb- und Bedürfnisausstattung verleugnen und den ihnen auferlegten Verzicht auf Glück und Genuss schließlich an sich selbst vollstrecken. Gleichzeitig, so setzt sich die Erzählung fort, verkommen Moral und Recht im bürgerlichen und mehr noch im nachbürgerlichen Zeitalter zu zynischen Herrschaftsinstrumenten, die nur den ökonomischen Profit moralisch bemänteln und die Verfolgung von Machtinteressen durch die herrschenden gesellschaftlichen Kräfte legalisieren sollen. Die Produkte der Unterhaltungsindustrie und Massenkultur propagieren wiederum konformistische Anpassung an das Bestehende und manipulieren die Subjekte in einer Weise, dass sie sich fungibel und kritiklos in die Reproduktion des Immergleichen einfügen." (Honneth & Sutterlüty, 2011, p. 71).

[14] An extensive description of how modernity has failed to fulfil its promises is given in Fromm (1979, p. 14).

society. Nowadays, Hartmut Rosa promotes such an understanding of sociology as a scientific discipline (2013; 2015a; 2016).[15] The idea that science should assist in the realization of a *good life* is a point for which Critical Theory is criticized – because how does one define a *good life*? According to which criteria, values, and justifications?

In the Frankfurt School, techno-scientific rationality, innovation, and ICT are interpreted as means of socio-political and economic power. Capitalism[16] is criticized as a source of alienation of the individual through work and cultural participation. The cultural industry is criticized insofar as the contentment associated with the consumption of cultural objects compensates for the alienating effects of labor. However, this compensatory Nature of cultural consumption would reinforce individual alienation. Therefore, the individual finds himself in a situation of double alienation through work and culture. This alienation forms the negative side of progress, which gives rise to skepticism about the project of modernity. **The Frankfurt School criticizes *traditional* science insofar as it neglects the techno-materialist, capitalist ideologies underlying scientific production, while *traditional* approaches criticize the Frankfurt School for its *a priori* Marxist ideologies.** [17] Critical Theory's interpretation of science leads to its designation as a normative science (Adorno, 2014/1951). Their epistemological differences lead to Habermas (1973/1968) criticizing science that aims to provide knowledge that is technically usable instead of being normative and ethically capable of guiding individuals (p.

---

[15] "Whether I choose to believe it or not, the ultimate objective of sociology, though rarely articulated (at least not consciously), is the question of the good life, or more precisely: the analysis of the social conditions under which a successful life is possible." (Rosa, 2015a, p. 67). See also the following quote regarding Rosa's view of the emergence of sociology: "In my view, sociology is born out of the diffuse but probably universal basic human perception that 'something is wrong here.' It is no coincidence that sociology as a scientific discipline emerges only in those places and times in which processes of modernisation visibly and palpably engulf people's immediate conditions of life. At the end of the nineteenth and the beginning of the twentieth centuries, when during industrialisation and urbanisation, the underlying tendencies of rationalisation, differentiation, domestication, and individualisation - in short, social 'acceleration' manifested beyond the level of the discursive and altered the modern form of life entirely" (Rosa, 2015a, p. 68). With "acceleration," Rosa refers to himself (see 2005; 2013). With the notion of "something is wrong here," Rosa refers to Boltanski & Chiapello (2011/1999).

[16] At the time of the birth of Critical Theory, the authors did not yet speak of *capitalism* but of an *advanced industrial society* (Habermas, 2013, p. 25).

[17] This argumentative circle is well summarised by Craig (1999, p. 149).

355).[18] The authors of the Frankfurt School show skepticism towards empirical theory, which emanates from their critique of quantifying principles that would initiate reification and alienation of the individual. Adorno criticizes the focus on method rather than reflexivity (1975/1966, p. 25), as well as simplifications and generalizations induced by positivist methods (ibid., p. 42). For Adorno, positivist thinking leads to the reification of thought and represents a submission to industrial processes. The question arises to what extent Critical Theory is a legitimate scientific approach regarding its prudence toward objectivity and neutrality. This point represents a major epistemological confrontation between *Critical Theory* and *traditional* science.

Let us follow Habermas (1973/1968) in his idea that a consequent epistemology can only be arrived at via an integral theory of society, and that a critique of the mechanisms of knowledge creation is not comprehensible other than through its societal context (ibid., p. 9). Habermas argues that the belief in techno-scientific rationality represents a certain human *interest,* and he points out that knowledge can also be created, for example, via the human body, affects, or introspection. What he criticizes is the dominance of techno-scientific rationality in Western societies over these alternative accesses to knowledge. Scientific knowledge would be widely considered the "only true knowledge" (ibid., p. 13). He argues that the interest in knowledge is itself motivated by affects – an idea taken from Nietzsche, who pointed out that rationality itself would be an expression of affects (ibid., p. 361). Habermas' approach is relevant to our investigation firstly because he understands interest as something outside of techno-scientific rationality,[19] and secondly, individual interest is conditioned by its cultural and socio-economic context. Thus, affects, conditioned by society, impact the direction of scientific research. Habermas (1974) criticizes *traditional* scientific culture insofar as it closes itself off to an epistemological critique of itself: positivism would only accept positivist arguments to self-

---

[18] See also the understanding of Doerre, Lessenich & Rosa (2015, p. 2), according to whom sociology: "... must always contain a critical analysis of the social relations of its time, and that the capitalist structure of its own society is to be placed center stage, as the analytical point of departure." Or, more precisely, Rosa (2015a, p. 67): "Whether I choose to believe it or not, the ultimate objective of sociology; though rarely articulated (at least not consciously), is the question of the good life, or more precisely: the analysis of the social conditions under which a successful life is possible."

[19] Note that Habermas (as well as other Frankfurt School authors) talks mostly about *drives – (Triebe)* – which is a German word rarely used today. Their perception of this word is included in our definition of *affects*.

criticize. A true critique, on the other hand, could be made only from a perspective outside of positivism:

"Only information that meets the criteria of empirical results can be considered as knowledge in the strict sense. Thus, a standard is established before the entire tradition sinks into mythology. With every scientific advance, archaic worldviews, religious beliefs, and philosophical interpretations lose ground. Cosmology and all the pre-scientific interpretations of the world that provide guidelines for action and justifications for norms lose their credibility to the same extent that a nature objectified in its causal links is recognized and subjected to the technical power of elimination." (Habermas, 1973/1968, p. 354).[20]

His perspective invites us to ask whether our research questions concerning the link between affects, the human body, design, and innovation may escape positivist epistemology and should rather be addressed by non-positivist or even non-scientific approaches. According to Habermas, the progressive domination of techno-scientific rationality leads to a negation of subjectivity and affect. (Subjectivity and affects are elements we identified in the previous chapters as constituting design competencies.) Habermas (1973/1968, p. 88, 153) notes that epistemological reflections tend to remain at the methodological level. But instead, science should be questioned as a whole. Nietzsche's critique of positivism goes even further insofar as he considers that the positivist approach implies the destruction of human knowledge by erasing historical, non-scientific knowledge (archaic, religious, spiritual, or astrological approaches). This critique relates to the ambiguity of modern progress, according to which the exploitation of Nature leads to an exploitation of humans themselves (See Marcuse, 1991/1964; or more recently: Han, 2013a; 2013b; 2019). Quantifying logic would be a gateway to the

---

[20] Our translation. Original text: "Allein die Informationen, die den Kriterien erfahrungswissenschaftlicher Resultate entsprechen, dürfen im strikten Sinne als Erkenntnis gelten. Damit wird ein Standard aufgerichtet, vor dem die Überlieferung insgesamt zur Mythologie herabsinkt. Mit jedem wissenschaftlichen Fortschritt verlieren die archaischen Weltbilder, die religiösen Anschauungen und philosophischen Deutungen an Boden. Kosmologie sowie alle vorwissenschaftlichen Weltinterpretationen, die Handlungsorientierungen und Rechtfertigungen von Normen ermöglichen, büßen in demselben Maße ihre Glaubwürdigkeit ein, als eine objektivierte Natur in ihren kausalen Zusammenhängen erkannt und der technischen Verfügungsgewalt unterworfen wird." (Habermas, 1973/1968, p. 354).

reification of the individual, which would then lead to alienation, as they would be in opposition to their anthropological Nature. For the Frankfurt School, this represents a major cause of modern societal pathologies.

Nowadays, design practices and innovation projects are key to what the Critical Theory refers to as *Industry*. As explained in the previous chapters, user research methods aim to understand modern individuals as precisely as possible. The user impacts the conception of innovations by being considered through user-centered approaches. Conversely, an innovation impacts the user through its possibilities and restraints of usage, creating feedback between innovations and users. Taking users into account facilitates and reinforces the synchronization between industrial processes and the anthropological complexity of the individual/user. The user-centered turn thereby radicalizes Horkheimer & Adorno's (2013/1947) interpretation of the involvement of individuals in industrial processes.

Regarding the involvement of user feedback in the development of new products or services, the Frankfurt School would state that the individual does not know his own need and that the integration of his opinions leads to more alienation. Technologies are developed according to the economic interests of the project owner, and affects are transformed into consumable goods via user research and design methods. Therefore, for the Frankfurt School, the user-centered turn would rather represent a euphemism. According to the Frankfurt School, the societal value of technology does not only depend on its use, but is already embedded in the process of its development. Innovations are not neutral or mere supports; they are already pre-decisions (Anders, 1985/1956), a form of socio-political power (Marcuse, 1991/1964), and ideology (Habermas, 1974). Put differently: an innovation expresses the ideology and interests of its creator and the era under which it is created:

> "The concept of technical reason is perhaps itself an ideology. Not only its use but already the technology is domination (over Nature and man), a methodical, scientific, calculated, and calculating domination. Certain goals and interests of domination are not only 'subsequently' and externally imposed on technology–they are already included in the construction of the technical apparatus itself; technology is, in each case, a social-historical project; it is projected what society and the interests that dominate it intend to do with people and things. Such a goal of domination is 'material' and thus belongs to the very form of

technical reason."[21] (Marcuse (1965) quoted in Habermas (1974, p. 50)).

Modernity and its psycho-somatic-affective ambiguities

Innovation – the improvement of existing products or the creation of new ones – is a major force underlying capitalism (Schumpeter, 2008/1942), promoting the acceleration of modernity (Rosa, 2005). According to Rosa (2018, p. 16), modernity is characterized by the need for exponential growth, necessitating permanent innovation. Design and innovation actors are, through their influences on the development of new products and services, key players in NPD processes and modernity more broadly (Reckwitz, 2019). At the heart of Rosa's acceleration is the techno-scientific progress pushed by the innovation sector, aiming at mastering Nature for the purpose of individual wellbeing, freedom, and emancipation. The dilemma of modernity, according to Hartmut Rosa, and what Critical Theory calls negative dialectic, is that modern societies try to make the world more accessible through science, technology, innovation, and design but paradoxically create the opposite effect: instead of feeling closer to the world and resonating with more things, modern individuals would feel more distant from the world and themselves. Put short: "Resonance is the promise of modernity; alienation is its reality" (Rosa, 2016, p. 624).[22] Thus,

---

[21] Our translation. Original text: "Der Begriff der technischen Vernunft ist vielleicht selbst Ideologie. Not erst ihre Verwendung, sondern schon die Technik ist Herrschaft (über die Natur und über den Menschen), methodische, wissenschaftliche, berechnete und berechnende Herrschaft. Bestimmte Zwecke und Interessen der Herrschaft sind nicht erst >nachträglich< und von außen der Technik oktroyiert - sie gehen schon in die Konstruktion des technischen Apparats selbst ein; Technik ist jeweils ein geschichtlich- gesellschaftliches Projekt; in ihr ist projektiert, was eine Gesellschaft und die sie beherrschenden Interessen mit den Menschen und mit den Dingen zu machen gedenken. Ein solcher Zweck der Herrschaft ist >material< und gehört insofern zur Form selbst der technischen Vernunft." (Marcuse (1965) quoted in Habermas (1974, p. 50)).

[22] Our translation. Original text: "Resonanz bleibt das Versprechen der Moderne, Entfremdung aber ist ihre Realität." (Rosa, 2016, p. 624). Or: "My thesis is that the institutionally achieved and culturally propagated promise of increasing the accessibility of the world not only does not 'work' but is self-defeating." Our translation. In original: "Meine These lautet, dass dieses institutionell erzwungene und kulturell als Verheißung und Versprechung fungierende Programm der Verfügbarmachung von Welt nicht nur 'funktioniert', sondern geradewegs in sein Gegenteil umschlägt." (Rosa, 2016, p. 25).

Hartmut Rosa continues the line of thought from Erich Fromm (1979). In the following section, I will link the previously described approach of the Frankfurt School to the psycho-somatic-affective disposition of individuals while indicating the role of modern design practices and the innovation sector.

The design of a given technology conditions the gestures through which it is used and, consequently, the human body. Through this, the UX-design of technologies impacts the psycho-somatic-affective disposition of users. For example, the way in which a button is pushed or a screen is used, the materials used, etc., condition small gestures that accumulate over time. Given the growing presence of ICT and digital innovation in private, professional, and public life, this effect is ever-growing. Adorno (2014/1951) criticizes the reductionist mechanization of users via gestures, and the following quote shows the radicality of his critique:

> "In the movements that machines demand of their operators, there is already a violent and striking expression of fascist abuse. The death of experience contributes to the fact that things take on a form that limits their manipulation to mere functional utility, without the additional freedom of behavior, nor of the autonomy of things, which would remain as the core of the experience, which would not be eliminated by the moment of action." (Adorno, 2014/1951, p. 44).[23]

The Frankfurt School previously indicated the operationalization of design through the alliance of science, industry, and economics (Benjamin, 2015/1936). Indeed, contemporary design practices are highly rationalized (Henke, 2021b). Nevertheless, they include a creative and artistic dimension, which is why design can be located in a field of tensions between artistic expressions and their industrial applications (Henke & Martin-Juchat, 2021), which even leads to a rapprochement between brands and artists (Henke & Martin-Juchat, 2023, in press). Overall, design practices in innovation projects

---

[23] Our translation. Original text: "In den Bewegungen, welche die Maschinen von den sie Bedienenden verlangen, liegt schon das Gewaltsame, Zuschlagende, stoßweise Unaufhörliche der faschistischen Misshandlungen. Am Absterben der Erfahrung trägt Schuld nicht zum letzten, daß die Dinge unterm Gesetz ihrer reinen Zweckmäßigkeit eine Form annehmen, die den Umgang mit ihnen auf bloße Handhabung beschränkt, ohne einen Überschuss, sei's an Freiheit des Verhaltens, sei's an Selbstständigkeit des Dinges zu dulden, der als Erfahrungskern überlebt, weil er nicht verzehrt wird vom Augenblick der Aktion." (Adorno, 2014/1951, p. 44).

are marked by a rationalization of creative forces and a reification of affects for mercantile purposes. Does the question arise whether this serves emancipation or alienation of users?

In Nietzsche's work, his approach to the human body resembles the idea of Embodiment, but it goes further. Nietzsche locates rationality, cognition, and consciousness in the human flesh. So far, the approach still reflects Embodiment, but then Nietzsche goes further: he attributes *more* wisdom and truth to the body than to rationality. This becomes clear with his following quote: "Behind your thoughts and feelings, my brother, there is a powerful ruler, an unknown sage – he is called Self. In your body, it dwells; your body it is. There is more reason in your body than in your best wisdom. And who knows why your body needs your best wisdom?."[24] **Nietzsche argues that the body is the source of affect, reflexivity, consciousness, and also of morality, beliefs, and ideologies, such as those of techno-scientific rationality. It is quite striking, then, to imagine that the values that lead the progress of modernity towards a decline of psycho-somatic-affective competencies would themselves be anchored in and motivated by the human body.**

To explain this, Nietzsche would say *motivated by an alienated body*–that the bodily motivations that condition modern values are those of an alienated body that does not express its true needs – which would be those of *increasing its power* (his famous term "Wille zur Macht" in the original). In terms of Critical Theory, design practices and innovation projects tend to reflect the modern negation of the corporality of an individual, leading through the diminution of psycho-somatic-affective capacities to alienation instead of emancipation. The intention to make Nature more comprehensible, accessible, and controllable through techno-scientific means causes the opposite effect – modern individuals would be alienated from Nature (Rosa, 2016). From such a perspective, the user-centered turn deployed in the innovation sector would indeed represent a euphemism. Nevertheless, the benefits of design and innovation are not negligible and account for impressive progress. Therefore, the approach of the Frankfurt School reveals foremost an ambiguity inherent to

---

[24] Our translation. Original text: "Hinter deinen Gedanken und Gefühlen, mein Bruder, steht ein mächtiger Gebieter, ein unbekannter Weiser - der heißt Selbst. In deinem Leibe wohnt er, dein Leib ist er. Es ist mehr Vernunft in deinem Leibe, als in deiner besten Weisheit. Und wer weiß denn, wozu dein Leib gerade deine beste Weisheit nötig hat?" (Nietzsche, 2019/1883, p. 31).

progress. Their approach indicates that with techno-scientific progress comes an amplification of the responsibilities of users and an increase in the importance of education for using innovation and ICT responsibly.

A critical approach to contemporary design practices and innovation projects

Referring to Walter Benjamin's work on art, Adorno (2007/1977, p. 119) notes: "Once again, I would like to emphasize the passage on the 'liberation of things from the slavery of utility' as a brilliant turning point for the dialectical salvation of the commodity."[25] What Adorno expresses in this idea, transposed to the contemporary innovation sector, indicates that the liberation of innovations from utility might eliminate their reifying and alienating character. But one of the objectives of innovation projects is exactly this – utility and usability. The absurdity carried by such an idea (liberating an innovation of its utility) indicates the gap between the values of the innovation sector and Critical Theory. It appears untenable in the face of the values of the innovation sector.

Today, the user is empowered by innovations and, at the same time, exploited by the interests of the project owners. Now, even without following a socio-technical determinism, technology would not be neutral because the psycho-somatic-affective disposition of the project owner and designer is inscribed in its conception and realization (whether implicitly or explicitly), which opens the door to a contemporary Critical Theory of the innovation sector. In particular, the rationalization, standardization, and functional reification that follow the operationalization of design practices, user affects, and the human body in the contemporary innovation sector represents an extension of the Frankfurt School's critique of cultural industries.

Positive valence and wellbeing, as well as increased efficiency and comfort, are dominant values in the innovation sector. In Business-to-Customer (B2C) innovation, wellbeing is often placed at the forefront to promote products.

---

[25] Our translation. Original text: "Once more, I should like to emphasize most strongly the passage about the 'liberation of things from the bondage of being useful' as a brilliant turning-point for the dialectical salvation of the commodity" (Adorno, 2007/1977, p. 119).

In Business-to-Business (B2B) innovation, this notion is rather indirectly implemented, for example, by augmenting the efficiency of industrial processes, increasing wages, saving time or money, and finally enhancing wellbeing.

In contrast to these values lies Nietzsche's approach, which I will outline in this section, transferring his deconstruction of ethical values, taken as immutable in modern Western societies, to the contemporary innovation sector. But before elaborating on this, I want to point out that design practices are built around two main dimensions. One is the aesthetic dimension – the objective is to create something that will be perceived as visually aesthetic and pleasing by the user. The other dimension is comprehension – the objective is to create something that communicates and transfers information in a functional way depending on the objectives of the project owner. The objective of design from the perspective of the project owner is to facilitate, through the aesthetic dimension, the understanding of a given content. In most cases, the aim of design practice is to create something aesthetic and understandable.

But producing something aesthetic is criticizable as it contains an underlying value system. *Why* create something aesthetic? Why wouldn't it be *better* to do the opposite? One might answer with the need to sell innovations (the functionalist side) or with the improvement of the habitability of the world (the hedonist side), but Nietzsche asks these questions to dismantle the Western system of values and morals. The paradigms of the innovation sector and of the user-centered turn would, for him, be idols and apriorism to be dismantled ("Götzen" in the original; see Nietzsche, 2019/1883; 2008/1889). According to him, aesthetic judgments imply an underlying morality and, therefore, can be seen as random and changeable. The form they take is linked to the sociogenesis of their respective cultures. Nietzsche deconstructs Socrates' triad of the beautiful, the true, and the good by insisting that truth is not necessarily either beautiful or good. This idea can be transferred to design practices, innovation projects, and the user-centered turn. Combining Nietzsche's thinking with the Frankfurt School, design and innovation rather serve to blind users to commercial interests as, for Nietzsche, it is not wellbeing that is desirable, but the increase of human power (psycho-somatic-affective competencies). Wellbeing, if depending on a reduction of the daily involvement of the human body, might rather have the opposite effect in the long run. This idea is formulated in Nietzsche's Genealogy of Morals:

"...until now, there has not been the slightest doubt or hesitation about the higher value of 'good' over 'bad' in terms of support, utility, and prosperity for a man (including the future of humanity). But how? What if the reverse were true? How could it be? What if there was a symptom of decline inherent in the good,' as well as a danger, a seduction, a poison, a drug through which the present lived at the expense of the future? Perhaps the expression of something more comfortable, less dangerous, but also in a more discreet style or at a lower level? So would this morality be to blame if the highest possible power and magnificence of the human race could never be achieved? In that case, would morality be the danger of danger?" (Nietzsche, 1967/1887, p. 181).[26]

What Nietzsche denounces in this quotation finds its counterpart in the belief in the techno-scientific progress of improvement manifested by contemporary innovations. **Accordingly, the activity of the innovation sector would be part of this *poison*, and innovations or designs to be regarded as a *narcotic*.** Nietzsche (1967, p. 27, p. 496) criticizes the increasing control over affects, the decreasing presentation of affects in the public space, and the growth of shame (Elias, 2013/1939) because this genesis would distance the individual from its anthropological Nature. The activity of the contemporary innovation sector can be regarded as an extension and reinforcement of this genesis. The usage of ICT, and in particular SNS, are marked by a mastery of the presentation of affects. Their presentation can be temporally and spatially decontextualized. This gap between their formation and presentation gives way to functional considerations of the presentation of the digital self and creates an operationalization of these affects. But for Nietzsche, affects are key to

---

[26] Our translation. Original text: "...man hat bisher auch nicht im entferntesten daran gezweifelt und geschwankt, 'den Guten' für höherwertig als 'den Bösen' anzusetzen, höherwertig im Sinne der Förderung, Nützlichkeit, Gedeihlichkeit in Hinsicht auf den Menschen überhaupt (die Zukunft des Menschen eingerechnet). Wie? wenn das Umgekehrte die Wahrheit wäre? Wie? wenn im 'Guten'" auch ein Rückgangssymptom läge, insgleichen eine Gefahr, eine Verführung, ein Gift, ein Narkotikum, durch das etwa die Gegenwart auf Kosten der Zukunft lebte? Vielleicht behaglicher, ungefährlicher, aber auch in kleinerem Stile, niedriger? ... So daß gerade die Moral daran schuld wäre, wenn eine an sich mögliche höchste Mächtigkeit und Pracht des Typeus Mensch niemals erreicht würde? So daß gerade die Moral die Gefahr der Gefahren wäre?" (Nietzsche, 1977/1887, p. 12). The suspension points at the start of the sentence were Nietzsche's.

knowledge (1967, p. 256). He took a holistic view of the human being by understanding him not only through his rationality but also through his affective complexity, inner conflicts, paradoxes, and inconsistencies – the forces that constitute the famous *Will to Power* (as mentioned earlier; "Wille zur Macht" in its original formulation). According to this thinking, a focus on rationality limits the individual in his bodily capacities and in the richness of its affects. The evolution of ICT from the 20th Century to the present day has been accompanied by a decrease in daily bodily activities. Considering Embodiment, it seems that techno-scientific progress diminishes psycho-somatic-affective competencies. This would be in line with Adorno's negative dialectic (1975/1966). **Expressing this through Offe's (2010) differentiation between *net* and *gross* progress, Nietzsche (1977/1887), as well as Adorno (1975/1966; 2014/1951), state that negative externalities (decreases in psycho-somatic-affective or ethical competencies) outweigh net progress (techno-scientific advancement), leading to negative *gross* progress. Thus, they are interpreted in the sense of regression rather than progress during modernity, and nowadays the innovation sector seems more occupied by net than gross progress.**

The ideology underlying the contemporary innovation sector still largely resembles that of a belief in techno-scientific rationality, criticized by the Frankfurt School. It implies that the future envisaged by techno-scientific progress would be desirable, ameliorative, and without alternative (Honneth, 2016/2007). But following Nietzsche's perspective, contemporary design and innovation activities would be more of a euphemism regarding the ecological crisis, the health crisis, the psychological crisis (the rise of pathologies such as burnout and depression), the vulnerability of systems (linked to the economic crisis) and of individuals (through precarity), as well as the amplification of the divide between rich and poor. Thus, the contemporary innovation sector is expanding to include social, responsible, ethical, and ecological innovations, through which it counterbalances its detrimental consequences. I like to ask whether it does this sufficiently. Does it fulfill its attributed socio-political responsibility? Or does it betray its promoting values to provide ameliorative progress?

The initial values of Silicon Valley, modern ICT development, and the contemporary innovation sector express a certain hope for human emancipation. According to Weber (2002/1905), Mumford (2000/1952), and Musso (2003), this hope is motivated by the same forces as religious and spiritual beliefs, and modernity would be characterized by a betrayal of its promises. The Critical

Theory of the Frankfurt School, and especially Adorno's negative dialectic, states that the idea of ameliorative progress would not be tenable according to the events of the 20th Century.[27] The central problem of his negative dialectic lies in the question of how the human being, being a potentially free subject, has become an object of its own power. His proposed answer is: via techno-scientific progress and its ambiguities. He argues that the benefits achieved by progress are negated by the unintended effects they imply (Adorno, 1975/1966). Human emancipation from Nature towards wellbeing and freedom would automatically imply the loss of this human Nature, thereby creating the socio-psychological pathologies of modernity. This dialectic is marked by a loss of resonance between the individual and the world (Rosa, 2013; 2016; 2018). In this view, the negative dialectic implies a psycho-somatic-affective degeneration of the modern individual. For this reason, Adorno speaks of the *negativity* of progress. This negativity does not only represent degeneration and destruction, but the necessity of socio-political power, and in modernity, this power would take the form of totalitarian techno-scientific rationality (Marcuse, 1991/1964). Adorno sees the source of the power of rationality in the language ("Begriff" in original formulation). Human beings would have begun to submit Nature to his thought at the cost of losing the initial identity of this Nature.

The origin of progress is, according to this approach, the emergence of language. The emergence of the communicative subjugation of Nature by man is, for Adorno, a response to a quest for identity. This aspect allows the imagination of alternatives, as there might be other solutions to socio-individual identity construction. Alternatives might become accessible by considering the human body as the origin of socio-individual identity. Hence, I propose to access the identity inquiry via the human body. The dilemma of the negative dialectic is the difficulty for the individual to emerge from his pathologies. According to Adorno's thinking, each emancipatory step would be an expression and reinforcement of alienating forces. I propose to solve this dilemma by complementing Critical Theory with Embodiment.[28] Critical Theory assumes that techno-scientific rationality is the only option for the modern

---

[27] For Adorno, the catastrophe of the Second World War is a revelation of this dilemma. Auschwitz is, for him, the consequence of progress where modernity as utopia is revealed as illusory. Another reason for Adorno's resignation is caused by the fact that all attempts to realise Marxism have failed.

[28] Varela, Thompson & Rosch (2016/1991) do this in a similar way in their approach to *Enactivism,* in which they combine cognitive science with phenomenology and Buddhism.

individual, which seems true, as it is profoundly embedded in Western societies, but thanks to globalization, alternatives to techno-scientific rationality have become more easily available. **Given that the starting point of Critical Theory's analyses is the over-identification of the modern individual with rational reflexivity independent of his or her body, the consideration of non-scientific approaches could complement these theories by proposing socio-psychological solutions, capable of resolving the dialectical dilemma of progress that Critical Theory is not able to provide.** There are some contributions in the work of negative dialectics which point in such a direction as the importance of spontaneity as a behavior that might solve modern pathologies (Adorno, 1975/1966). Spontaneity would require social trust and openness, and it is key to enabling experiences of resonance between the individual and the world (Rosa, 2016). Developing such a psycho-somatic-affective state represents an educational task.

The Embodiment perspective related to the Human-Computer Interaction (HCI) context reinforces the importance of considering the perceptual situations and materialities of ICT. Therefore, there is a certain collision of Embodiment with the promotional discourse of ICT. Embodiment is a perspective that emphasizes the physical side of an experience in real space and time – here and now – while the promotional discourse of innovations and ICTs emphasizes the liberation from geographical and temporal restrictions. I propose that taking the human body into account as an emancipatory means might allow what Adorno's negative dialectic does not achieve – the liberation of the individual from socio-psychological pathologies. This becomes possible through Embodiment, which anchors the individual's cognition and consciousness in the human body, and which allows educational and emancipatory access to respond to pathologies. Considering that human existence is primarily corporal, the consideration of the human body closes a blind spot in the approaches of the Frankfurt School authors, since they did not consider the corporality of the individual as a potential way out of pathologies.

Conclusion

This chapter introduced the Frankfurt School approach by situating it in its historical and socio-political context, highlighting the epistemological differences between Critical Theory and traditional theory, and applying Critical Theory to the contemporary innovation sector. Major economic forces identified by the first generation of Frankfurt School thinkers – the ubiquity of ICT, capitalist mechanisms, and the alliance between technology, science, and industry – remain key drivers of the contemporary innovation sector. Based on this perspective, I have shed light on the feedback between the user, innovation, and designer. We have seen some of the epistemological and socio-psychological features of design that pose challenges to the operationalization of design in innovation projects, and explored how design can be located in a field of tensions between artistic expressions and their applications in mercantile contexts through functionalist rationalizations.

The approach of the Frankfurt School needs to be analyzed in its cultural and historical context during and after the Second World War.[29] It does not apply identically today because of the socio-economic progress that has taken place since then, and a re-conceptualization of their approach is needed to adapt it to the configuration of the 21st Century (Honneth, 2016/2007, p. 56). The contemporary socio-economic context does not represent the precarity as it was during the time of Marx or the Frankfurt School; on the contrary, it is rather marked by materialist abundance. Nevertheless, fundamental principles remain identifiable in the innovation sector. Honneth & Sutterlüty (2011) explain that the contemporary approach of the Frankfurt School is more moderate than that of the first-generation thinkers. Nevertheless, the Frankfurt School still follows the "normative paradoxes" approach (ibid., p. 69), which is not only concerned with the uncertainties but the ambivalences of modernity. The positioning of the Frankfurt School today distances itself from one-sided criticisms of the first generation of Critical Theory.[30] Today, the benefits of techno-scientific progress are more visible. Therefore, I ask to what extent the analysis of modernity in the form of a collective pathology is a form of hypochondria. Do the benefits of techno-scientific progress justify the non-intended consequences? Or is the user-centered turn a euphemism?[31] Combining Adorno's (1975/1966) perspective

---

[29] World War II and the concentration camps are explicitly mentioned in Adorno's work. He attributes Auschwitz the status of a metaphysical fact from which the dialectical Nature of human history is revealed.

[30] http://www.ifs.uni-Frankfurt.de/forschung/

[31] It is similar to Nietzsche's line of thought: "O *sancta simplicitas!* What a strange simplification and falsification man lives in! One cannot help but wonder once one has laid eyes on this wonder! How I have made everything around us bright, free and light, and

with Offe's (2010), Adorno's negative dialectic represents the idea that while an increase in *gross* progress (techno-scientific advancement) may be in evidence, taking into account negative externalities (psychosocial pathologies and decreases in psycho-somatic-affective competencies) can actually mean a decrease in *net* progress.

---

simple! How I have given our senses free passage to all superficial things, to give our thinking a divine desire for free impulses and false conclusions! – How I understood from the beginning that I had to let our ignorance, our recklessness, our heart, our joy of living enjoy life! And it is only on this now solid and granite soil of ignorance that science has so far been able to rise, the will to know on the ground of a much more powerful will, the will to not know, to be uncertain, to be false! Not as its opposite, but - as its refinement!" Our translation from the original text: *"O sancta simplicitas!* In welcher seltsamen Vereinfachung und Fälschung lebt der Mensch! Man kann sich nicht zu Ende wundern, wenn man sich erst einmal die Augen für dies Wunder eingesetzt hat! How I have all things that are safe and free and easy and simple to understand! How I have been able to make our souls free for all things above ground, our thoughts and dreams a joyful beginning after many turns of the road and many setbacks! - wie haben wir es von Anfang an verstanden, uns uns unsre Unwissenheit, Unvorsichtigkeit, Herzhaftigkeit, Heiterkeit des Lebens, um das Leben zu genießen! Und erst auf diesem nunmehr festen und granitnen Grunde von Unwissenheit durfte sich bisher die Wissenschaft erheben, der Wille zum Wissen auf dem Grunde eines viel gewaltigeren Willens, des Willens zum Nicht-wissen, zum Ungewissen, zum Unwahren! Not as sein Gegensatz, sondern - as seine Verfeinerung!" (Nietzsche, 1967, p. 29).

Towards a responsible design

In this chapter, I discuss the role of design and innovation in the upcoming years. Crucial points are Artificial Intelligence (AI), the Internet of Things (IoT), the participation of design in political discourses, and the development of an adequate innovation ethic. As future-oriented, ameliorative activities, design, and innovation express tendentious conceptualization and can therefore be criticized. They are drivers of economic development and political issues. Today's highly diversified and rationalized design practices are meant to justify their existence by profitability. In saying this, I leave aside forms of "authorial design" (according to Zacklad, 2017). Designers work in multidisciplinary teams, close to communication professions. I assume that the streamlining of design will accelerate with AI. In particular, the technical quality of design practices will be pushed by AI, and especially aspects of design that follow causal logic will thereby be replaced. Similarly, in creativity, AI advances rapidly (Mazzone & Elgammal, 2019).[32] Faced with AI, one human advantage is to create things that *escape* causal logic, since the aspects of design that *follow* causal logic can more efficiently be done by AI. As soon as the project owner hires a human designer, his acausal creative forces represent a higher potential for the project owner – especially to achieve something *new*.

Today, design is often not done by designers but by other communication professions, facilitated by the operationalization of design and creativity (Henke, 2021b), as well as by the democratization of design tools. The Adobe Creative Suit gives cheap and relatively easy access to unlimited possibilities of audio-visual, visual, and auditory manipulations. I predict that design professions and other communication professions will evolve in the direction of cooperation until a quasi-merger (Henke & Martin-Juchat, 2021). In the meantime, the artistic side and the creative forces remain a phenomenon that is not yet sufficiently explained and that deserves more research: despite all efforts, creative forces remain an unclear anthropological phenomenon (Tan, 2000, p. 130).

---

[32] The replacement of creativity by AI remains a delicate issue–the question of how far creativity by AI represents *true* creativity or how far it is a human privilege is a debate that is not over. Either way, designers need to position themselves in relation to AI.

Despite a potential fusion with other communicative professions and AI, design practices will not lose their socio-political responsibility; rather, they will be amplified by the increasing weight of design in industrial processes. To cope with the increasing socio-economic importance of design and the resulting societal responsibility, I assert that design should participate more explicitly in political discourses. Norman (2013/1988, p. 293) reminds us that design faces the risk of being reduced to an external cosmetic: "The design of everyday things is in great danger of becoming the design of superfluous, overloaded, unnecessary things." Counteracting this trend and participating in socio-political discourses in a responsible and sustainable way remains a challenge for designers. Design has a responsibility to stimulate ideas, utopial developments, and societal discourses about the future (Dunne & Raby, 2013, p. 9). The responsibility of design in innovation projects becomes even more important if considering its links with affects and their corporality, as I have shown in this book.

Design practices and innovation projects impact psycho-somatic-affective structures and social interactions. The COVID-19 crisis and its socio-technological implications intensify the importance of innovations (especially ICT) in private, professional, and public life (Bar Am et al., 2020). User-centered approaches seem benevolent, but find their limits via the domination of techno-scientific rationality, which may be criticized in the face of their psycho-somatic-affective ambiguities. The non-fulfillment of the Silicon Valley values reminds us that design and innovation are subject to political interests, showing ambivalent effects on society. Thus, design practices and innovation projects need to be exposed to political debate. This debate, as well as the core of our research questions, are political and philosophical questions about the conceptualization of society and the future. [33] According to Habermas

---

[33] "If the phenomenon on which Marcuse fixes his social analysis, the particular fusion of technology and power, of rationality and oppression, could only be interpreted in the fact that in the material a priori of science and technology, there is a worldview determined by class interests and the historical situation, a 'project', as Marcuse puts it after the phenomenological Sartre–in that case, an emancipation would be unthinkable without a revolution of science and technology itself." Our translation. Original text: "Wenn das Phänomen, an dem Marcuse seine Gesellschaftsanalyse festmacht, eben die eigentümliche Verschmelzung von Technik und Herrschaft, Rationalität und Unterdrückung, nicht anders gedeutet werden könnte als dadurch, daß im materialen a priori von Wissenschaft und Technik ein durch Klasseninteresse und geschichtliche Situation bestimmter Weltentwurf, ein 'Projekt', wie Marcuse im Anschluß an den phänomenologischen Sartre sagt, steckt - dann wäre eine Emanzipation nicht

(1973/1968, p. 118; 1974, p. 54), this debate should take place outside of science. Taking non-scientific approaches into account might reduce the ambiguities inherent to progress.

Values promoting the contemporary innovation sector can be interpreted as a form of religious belief motivated by the hope of improving the quality of life through the increase in techno-scientific power over Nature (Mumford, 2000/1952; Gasset, 1952/1942). In the past, this promise has never been fulfilled (Fromm, 1979), and today there are no indications that the upcoming techno-scientific development of the 21st Century will be qualitatively different from the past. Even if one considers the exponential technological acceleration via, for example, AI or Bio-Computing, which may allow unforeseen achievements, Rosa states: "Of course, technological inventions will give us faster tools and further increase the speed of social life – but no one believes that this will put an end to the scarcity of time. Scientific innovations and political reforms will come about at a relentless pace – but no one really believes that these will improve our lives." (Rosa, 2015b, p. 288).

The alliance between science, technical application, and industrial exploitation follows an ethic, according to Gehlen (2007/1957, p. 60), that is not adequate to their societal impacts. Therefore, developing an adequate design and innovation ethic appears to be an essential challenge for the future. [34] Approaches to ecological, social, and responsible innovation do exist, but the question is whether their societal impact will be great enough to offset detrimental consequences. To envisage an ecologically and psycho-somatic-effective sustainable future, it is necessary to understand how ethics are involved in design practices and innovation projects. Design and innovation must be justified in the face of radical critique. The operationalizations of affects and their corporality in the design and innovation sector are even more criticizable by imagining the opportunity costs: if these creative forces are invested in innovation projects for mercantile purposes, they are not invested elsewhere – which alternatives would these creative energies hold?

---

zu denken ohne eine Revolutionierung von Wissenschaft und Technik selber." (Habermas, 1974, p. 54).

[34] Such a request is also made by Ménissier (2021).

Conclusion

Design and innovation represent not only a modern socio-economic paradigm but a fascinating anthropological phenomenon that shapes contemporary societies. The socio-economic importance of design practices and innovation projects have increased with the tertiarization and saturation of Western economies, and the contemporary innovation sector is still situated on a key dynamic of modernity: the alliance between science, industry, and technology (Habermas, 1974). In particular, ICT innovations restructure societies and create a state of ubiquitous and permanent connectivity (Vorderer, 2015).

The metaphysical values promoting the development of innovations (explicit or implicit) serve to justify their social integration. But despite their promotional values, innovations involve psycho-somatic-affective ambiguities (Martin-Juchat, Pierre & Dumas, 2015) and unintended effects (Fromm, 1979), which even seem to oppose the initial values (Flichy, 2003; Cardon, 2015). To understand these ambiguities more precisely, I have attempted to shed light on design practices and the functioning of innovation projects. Practitioners attribute little importance to the human body in their practices. They attribute great importance to affects, but do not integrate them explicitly (or, at least, only rarely). Affects are rather an implicit background layer (Henke, 2021a; 2021b).

I have identified design practices as semiotic concretizations through a tacit dialogue between the involved psycho-somatic-effective structures. Design serves to concretize content into the semiotic specificities of a given medium (for example, film or illustrations). By doing this, the content becomes more precise. This process includes a dialogue between a multitude of involved tools, materialities, and actors – the user, among others – which I defined as psycho-somatic-affective structures through the perspective of Embodiment (Niedenthal, 2007). Their dialogue mostly takes place in a tacit way (Polanyi, 1966/2009). Meanwhile, design contains socio-psychological and epistemological features (Gentes, 2017), which represent challenges for innovation management (Rammert et al., 2018). These features are found in the face of other communication professions and their mercantile context, and thus design can be located in a field of tensions between artistic expressions and their applications in industrial contexts.

The innovation sector operationalizes design for its ability to impact the ontological, pragmatic, prescriptive, and affective dimensions of communication in a tacit way, which represents advantages in saturated economies. Innovation projects operationalize design practices to address the different dimensions of communication – in other words: to speak more effectively to an individual/user. Therefore, the operationalization of design is part of the pervasive modern aestheticization (Michaud, 2011/2003) and represents the application of creative forces to mercantile ends (Benjamin, 2015/1936). As such, I have questioned the societal role of design practices and innovation projects through a Critical Theory.

The contemporary innovation sector predominantly expresses *a prioris* in ameliorative progress via techno-scientific rationality (Habermas, 1974; 2013). This allows impressive innovations and, at the same time, implies socio-psychological ambiguities (Fromm, 1979; Han, 2019), as modern innovations come at the cost of decreasing psycho-somatic-affective capacities externalized in these innovations. A program to counterbalance such effects could consist of emancipation through psycho-somatic-affective education, for example, proposed by Martin-Juchat (2020). Therefore, I complimented the Frankfurt School with Embodiment, closing a blind spot of Critical Theory. The Frankfurt School authors indicated that the ideologies of creators are inscribed in their creations, meaning that the values (implicit or explicit) of project owners are inscribed in innovations. These innovations affect private, professional, and public life (Vorderer, 2015) and are, therefore, not a neutral but a political issue (Ménissier, 2021). According to Critical Theory, the operationalizations of design practices in innovation projects can be interpreted as reinforcing the reification of the individual. Design and innovation represent a political issue, are negotiable, and need a societal discourse as they are conceptualizations about society and progress. The discussion of their societal role is far from being over – this book hopefully stimulates this discourse.

"Because the essence of technology is nothing technological, essential reflection upon technology and decisive confrontation with it must happen in a realm that is, on the one hand, akin to the essence of technology and, on the other, fundamentally different from it. Such a realm is art."

(Heidegger, 2013/1954, p. 35)

Bibliography

Adorno, T. (1975). *Negative Dialektik [Negative Dialectics]*. Frankfurt a.M.: Suhrkamp (1st ed. 1966).

Adorno, T. (1992). *Ästhetische Theorie [Aesthetic Theory]*. Frankfurt a.M.: Suhrkamp (1st ed. 1973).

Adorno, T. (2007). Letters to Walter Benjamin. In T. Adorno, T. Benjamin, T. Bloch, B. Brecht, & G. Lukács, *Aesthetics and Politics* (pp. 110-133). London: Verso (1st ed. 1977).

Adorno, T. (2014). *Minima Moralia. Reflexionen aus dem beschädigten Leben [Minima Moralia. Reflections from the damaged life]*. Frankfurt a.M.: Suhrkamp (1st ed. 1951).

Akrich, M. (1990). From the sociology of techniques to a sociology of uses: The impossible integration of the VCR in first generation cable networks. *Techniques et culture*, 83-110.

Alloing, C., & Pierre, J. (2017). *Le web affectif. Une économie numérique des émotions [The affective web. A digital economy of emotions]*. Bru-Sur-Marne: INA.

Anders, G. (1985). *Die Antiquiertheit des Menschen. Bd I. Über die Seele im Zeitalter der zweiten industriellen Revolution [The antiquity of man. Vol I. About the soul in the age of the second industrial revolution]*. München: Beck (1st ed. 1956).

Barsalou, L. (2008). Grounded Cognition. *Annual Review of Psychology, 59*, 617-645.

Bar Am, J., Furstenthal, L., Jorge, F., & Roth, E. (2020, 10 22). *Innovation in a crisis: Why it is more critical than ever. Priotizing innovation today is the key to unlocking postcrisis growth*. Retrieved from McKinsey & Company: https://www.mckinsey.com/~/media/McKinsey/Business%20Functions/St rategy%20and%20Corporate%20Finance/Our%20Insights/Innovation%2 0in%20a%20crisis%20Why%20it%20is%20more%20critical%20than%2 0ever/Innovation-in-a-crisis-Why-it-is-more-critical-than-ever-vF.pdf

Benjamin, W. (2015). *Das Kunstwerk im Zeitalter seiner technischen Reproduzierbarkeit [The Work of Art in the Age of its Technical Reproducibility].* Berlin: Suhrkamp (1st ed. 1936).

Breton, P., & Proulx, S. (1996). *L'explosion de la communication [The communication explosion].* Paris: La Découverte.

Cannon, W. B. (1929). Organization of physiologic homeostasis. *Physiological Reviews*, 9, 399-427.

Cardon, D. (2010). *La démocratie Internet. Promesses et limites [Internet democracy. Promises and limits].* Paris: Seuil.

Cardon, D. (2015). *À quoi rêvent les algorithms. Nos vies à l'heure des big data [What algorithms dream of. Our lives in the age of big data].* Paris: Seuil.

Certeau, M. (1990). *L'invention du quotidien. 1. arts de faire [The invention of everyday life. 1. arts of making].* Paris: Gallimard.

Cole, T., & Urchs, O. (2015). *Digital Enlightenment Now! How the Internet is making us better and smarter and in the process changing just about everything around us!* Lungau: Forsthaus.

Craig, R. T. (1999). Communication Theory as a Field. *Communication Theory, 9 (2)*, 119-161.

CRS (2020, 04 29). *Global Research and Development Expenditures: Fact Sheet.* Retrieved from Congressional Research Service: https://fas.org/sgp/crs/misc/R44283.pdf

Damasio, A. (2018). *The Strange Order of Things. Life, Feeling, and the Making of Cultures.* NY: Pantheon Books.

Doerre, K., Lessenich, S., & Rosa, H. (2015). *Sociology, Capitalism, Critique.* London: Verso (1st ed.: Soziologie - Kapitalismus - Kritik: Eine Debatte [Sociology - Capitalism - Criticism: A debate]. Suhrkamp. Translated by Jan-Peter Herrmann and Loren Balhorn).

Dourish, P. (2001). *Where the Action Is. The Foundations of Embodied Interaction.* Cambridge: MIT Press.

Dutta, S., Lanvin, B., & Wunsch-Vincent, S. (2020). *Global Innovation Index 2020. Who Will Finance Innovation?* Geneva, NY, Fontainebleau: Cornwell University, INSEAD, WIPO.

Dunne, A. (2006). *Hertzian Tales. Electronic Products, Aesthetic Experience, and Critical Design.* Cambridge: MIT Press.

Dunne, A., & Raby, F. (2013). *Speculative Everything. Design, Fiction, and Social Dreaming.* Cambdridge: MIT Press.

Ekman, p. (2014). *Gefühle lesen. Wie Sie Emotionen erkennen und richtig interpretieren [Read the feelings. How to recognize and correctly interpret emotions].* Heidelberg: Spektrum.

Elias, N. (2013). *Über den Prozess der Zivilisation. Soziogenetische und Psychogenetische Untersuchungen [About the process of civilization. Sociogenetic and psychogenetic studies].* Frankfurt a.M.: Suhrkamp (1st ed. 1939).

Findeli A. (2005) La recherche projet: une méthode pour la recherche en design [Project research: a method for design research], in Michel, R. (ed.), *Erstes Designforschungssymposium/First Design Research Symposium.* Zurich: SwissDesignNetwork, pp. 40-51. http://projekt.unimes.fr/files/2014/04/Findeli.2005.Recherche-projet.pdf

Flichy, P. (1997). *Une histoire de la communication modern. Espace public et vie privée [A history of modern communication. Public space and private life].* Paris: La Découverte (1st ed. 1991).

Flichy, P. (2003). *L'innovation technique. Récents développements en sciences sociales. Vers une nouvelle théorie de l'innovation [Technical innovation. Recent developments in social sciences. Towards a new theory of innovation].* Paris: Éditions la Découverte.

Franck, G. (1998). *Ökonomie der Aufmerksamkeit. Ein Entwurf [Economics of attention. A plan].* München: Hanser.

Frijda, N. (1986). *The Emotions.* Cambridge: CUP.

Fromm, E. (1979). *Haben oder Sein: Die seelischen Grundlagen einer neuen Gesellschaft [To have or to be: the mental foundations of a new society].* München: DTV.

Fromm, E. (1991). *Anatomie der menschlichen Destruktivität [Anatomy of human destructiveness].* Hamburg: Rororo (translated from the American by Mickel, L. & Mickel, E., 1st ed. 1973).

Fromm, E. (2006). *Die Pathologie der Normalität: Zur Wissenschaft vom Menschen [The Pathology of Normality: On Human Science]*. Berlin: Ullstein (1st ed. 2005).

Fuchs, C. (2020). *Kommunikation und Kapitalismus. Eine kritische Theorie [Communication and capitalism. A critical theory]*. München: UVK Verlag.

Gasset, J. (1952). *Das Wesen geschichtlicher Krisen [The nature of historical crises]*. Stuttgart: Deutsche Verlags Anstalt (1st ed. 1942).

Gavard-Perret, M., Gotteland, D., Haon, C., & Jolibert, A. (2018). *Méthodologie de la recherche en sciences de gestion [Research methodology in management sciences]*. Vol. 3. Montreuil: Pearson.

Gehlen, A. (2007). *Die Seele im technischen Zeitalter. Sozialpsychologische Probleme in der industriellen Gesellschaft [The soul in the technical age. Sociopsychological Problems in Industrial Society]*. Frankfurt a.M.: Klostermann GmbH (1st ed. 1957).

Gehlen, A. (2009). *Der Mensch: Seine Natur und seine Stellung in der Welt [Man: His nature and his position in the world]*. Wiebelsheim: Aula (1st ed. 1940).

Gentes, A. (2017). *The In-Discipline of Design. Bridging the Gap Between Humanities and Engineering*. Cham: Springer.

Gerrig, R., & Zimbardo, P. (2008). Emotionen, Stress, Gesundheit [Emotions, stress, health]. In Gerrig, R. & Zimbardo, P., *Psychology/Psychology* (pp. 454-467). London: Pearson.

Glennie, A., & Bound, K. (2016). *How Innovation Agencies Work: International lessons to inspire and inform national strategies*. London: Nesta.

Habermas, J. (1973). *Erkenntnis und Interesse [Knowledge and Interest]*. Frankfurt a.M.: Suhrkamp (1st ed. 1968).

Habermas, J. (1974). *Technik und Wissenschaft als "Ideologie" [Technology and Science as "Ideology"]*. Frankfurt a.M.: Suhrkamp.

Habermas, J. (2013). *Im Sog der Technokratie [In the wake of technocracy]*. Frankfurt a.M.: Suhrkamp.

Han, B. (2013a). *Transparenzgesellschaft [Transparency society]*. Berlin: Matthes-Seitz.

Han, B. (2013b). *Im Schwarm: Ansichten des Digitalen [In the Swarm: Views from the Digital].* Berlin: Matthes-Seitz.

Han, B. (2019). *Vom Verschwinden der Rituale. Eine Topologie der Gegenwart [The disappearance of rituals. A topology of the present].* Berlin: Ullstein.

Heidegger, M. (1963). *Sein und Zeit [Being and Time].* Tübingen: Max Niemeyer Verlag (1st ed. 1927).

Heidegger, M. (2013). *The Question Concerning Technology.* Translated by William Lovitt. NY: Harper Perennial Modern Thought (1st ed. 1954).

Henke, N. (2021a). The Corporality of Affects according to Design in Innovation Projects: Critical Approach, Analysis of Practices, and Perspectives. Thesis at University of Grenoble Alpes. http://www.theses.fr/2021GRALL017/document

Henke, N. (2021b). Design Methods and Innovation Agencies as Creativity Consultancy. *Revue Française des Sciences de l'Information et de la Communication, 23.* 16.

Henke, N. (2022). Corporal Implications of Design Practices and Methods. *Approches Théoriques en Information-Communication (ATIC),* 4, 73-81. https://doi.org/10.3917/atic.004.0073

Henke, N., & Martin-Juchat, F. (2021). The Design Turn for the Management of Public Relations: Emerging Challenges for Communication Professions. *ESSACHESS - Journal for Communication Studies, 14*(1), 22.

Henke, N. & Martin-Juchat. F. (2023, in press). The Alliance between Artists and Brands: Shared Interests and Limits of Design Processes. *KAIROS: the artist in the age of brands.* SFSIC.

Hochschild, A. (2012). *The Managed Heart. Commercialization of Human Feeling.* London: University of California Press (1st ed. 1983).

Honneth, A. & Sutterlüty, F. (2011). Normative Paradoxien der Gegenwart - eine Forschungsperspektive [Normative paradoxes of the present–a research perspective]. *WestEnd. Neue Zeitschrift für Sozialforschung.* Vol. 8 (1). p. 67-85.

Honneth, A. (2016). *Pathologien der Vernunft. Geschichte und Gegenwart der Kritischen Theorie [Pathologies of reason. The history and present of critical theory].* Frankfurt a.M.: Suhrkamp (1st ed. 2007).

Horkheimer, M., & Adorno, T. (2013). *Dialektik der Aufklärung [Dialectics of the Enlightenment].* Frankfurt a.M.: Fischer (1st ed. 1947).

Illouz, E. (2006). *Les sentiments du capitalisme [The sentiments of capitalism].* Paris: Seuil.

IXIADE. (2020). *White paper. A short treatise on the 10 major pitfalls of innovation.* Retrieved on 08 2020, from https://www.IXIADE.com/wp-content/uploads/2020/07/LIVRE-BLANC_FR_leaflet_4pages_200507-2.pdf

James, W. (1950). *The principles of psychology.* NY: Dover Publications (1st ed. 1890).

Jaruzelski, B., Chwalik, R., & Goehle, B. (2020, 10 03). *What the Top Innovators get Right.* Retrieved from Strategy+Business: https://www.strategy-business.com/feature/What-the-Top-Innovators-Get-Right?gko=e7cf9

Jay. M. (2018). *Dialektische Phantasie. Die Geschichte der Frankfurter Schule und des Instituts für Sozialforschung. 1923-1950 [Dialectical imagination. The History of the Frankfurt School and the Institute for Social Research. 1923-1950].* Frankfurt a.M.: Fischer (1st ed. 1973).

Katz, E., Blumler, J. G., & Gurevitch, M. (1974). Utilization of mass communication by the individual. In J. G. Blumler, & E. Katz (Eds.), *The uses of mass communications: Current perspectives on gratifications research* (pp. 19-32). Beverly Hills: Sage.

Keen, A. (2013). *The Cult of the Amateur.* London: Penguin.

Kelley, T. (2001). *The Art of Innovation. Lessons in Creativity from IDEO America's Leading Design Firm.* NY: Doubleday.

Kim, H.-C. (2015). Acceptability engineering: the study of user acceptance of innovative technologies. *Journal of Applied Research and Technology, 13*, 230-237.

Klimmt, C., Hefner, D., Reinecke, L., Rieger, D., & Vorderer, p. (2018). The permanently online and permanently connected mind: Mapping the cognitive structures behind mobile internet use. In D. Hefner, L. Reinecke, & C. Klimmt, *Permanently online, permanently connected. Living and communicating in a POPC world* (pp. 18-28). New York, NY: Routledge.

Kotler, P., Kartajaya, H. & Setiawan, I. (2021). *Marketing 5.0: Technology for Humanity*. NJ: Wiley.

Kramer, A., Guillory, J., & Hancock, J. (2014). Experimental evidence of massive-scale emotional contagion through social networks. *PNAS, 111*(24), 8788-8790.

Lanier, J. (2014). *Who owns the Future?* London: Penguin.

Lazarsfeld, P., Berelson, B. & Gaudet, H. (1944). *The People's Choice: How The Voter Makes Up His Mind in a Presidential Campaign*. NY: Columbia University Press.

Le Breton, D. (2015). *Anthropologie du corps et modernité [Anthropology of the body and modernity]*. Paris: PUF (1st ed. 1990).

Leitan, N. D., & Chaffey, L. (2014). Embodied Cognition and its applications: A brief review. *Journal of Mind, Brain & Culture*.

Lépine, V. (2015). Mesures et évaluation de la communication interne : quelles pratiques et quels enjeux ? [Measurement and evaluation of internal communication: what practices and what issues?] *Sociologies pratiques/ Practical sociologies*. 30. 10.3917/sopr.030.0053.

Lépine, V., Martin-Juchat, F.; Ménissier, T. (2018). *Improvisation et communication ou l'art de travailler ensemble autrement : l'expérimentation Org'impro [Improvisation and communication or the art of working together differently: the Org'impro experiment]*. hal-0184617

Lévy, p. (2018). *Le temps de l'expérience. Enchanter le quotidien par le design [The time of experience. Enchanting the everyday through design]* (HDR). Paris: utc.

Lieberman, D. (2013). *The Story of the Human Body*. London: Penguin Books.

Lipovetsky, G., & Serroy, J. (2013). *L'Esthétisation du monde. Vivre à l'âge du capitalisme artiste [The Aesthetization of the World. Living in the age of artist capitalism]*. Paris: Gallimard.

Mai, L., Freudenthaler, R., Schneider, F., & Vorderer, p. (2015). "I know you've seen it!" Individual and social factors for users' chatting behavior on Facebook. *Computers in Human Behavior, 49*, 296-302.

Mallein, P. & Toussaint, Y. (1994). L'intégration sociale des TIC : une sociologie des usages [The social integration of ICT: a sociology of uses]. *Information Technology and Society,* 6(4): 315-335.

Marcuse, H. (1965). *Kultur und Gesellschaft II [Culture and Society II].* Frankfurt a.M.: Suhrkamp.

Marcuse, H. (1969). *Versuch über die Befreiung [Attempt at Liberation].* Frankfurt a.M.: Suhrkamp.

Marcuse, H. (1991). *One-Dimensional Man. Studies in the Ideology of Advanced Industrial Society (2nd ed.).* Boston: Beacon Press (1st ed. 1964).

Martin-Juchat, F. (2002). Anthropologie du corps communicant [Anthropology of the communicating body]. *Mediation et information, L'Harmattan,* 12.

Martin-Juchat, F. (2008a). *Le corps et les médias: La chair éprouvée par les médias et les espaces sociaux [The body and the media: The flesh tested by the media and social spaces].* Grenoble: Presses Universitaires de Grenoble.

Martin-Juchat, F. (2008b). Penser le corps affectif comme un média dans une perspective d'anthropologie par la communication [Thinking of the affective body as a medium in a perspective of anthropology through communication]. *Revue Le corps, 4,* 85-92.

Martin-Juchat, F. (2013). Capitalisme affectif : enjeux et pratiques dans les organisations [Affective capitalism: issues and practices in organizations]. In Parrini-Alemanno, *Communications, organisationnelles, Management et numérique* (p. 6). Paris: L'Harmattan.

Martin-Juchat, F. (2014). La dynamique de la marchandisation de la communication affective [The dynamics of the commodification of affective communication]. *Revue française des sciences de l'information et de la communication, 5.*

Martin-Juchat, F., Pierre, J., & Dumas, A. (2015). Distraction and Boredom: Students Faced to Digital Economy. *Studies in Media and Communication, 3*(1), 134-143.

Martin-Juchat, F., & Staii, A. (2016). *L'industrialisation des émotions. Vers une radicalisation de la modernité ? [The industrialization of emotions. Towards a radicalisation of modernity?].* Paris: L'Harmattan.

Martin-Juchat, F. (2020). *L'aventure du corps. La communication corporelle, une voie vers l'émancipation [The adventure of the body. Body communication, a way to emancipation]*. Grenoble: PUG.

Mattelart, A. (2011). *L'invention de la communication [The invention of communication]*. Paris: La Découverte.

Mauss, M. (1934). Les techniques du corps [Body techniques]. *Journal of Psychology*, 23.

Mazzone, M., & Elgammal, A. (2019). Art, Creativity, and the Potential of Artificial Intelligence. *Arts*, 8(26).

McLuhan, M. (2001). *The Medium is the Massage. An Inventory of Effects*. Hong Kong: Gingko Press (1st ed. 1967).

Ménissier, T. (2016). Innovation et histoire. Une critique philosophique [Innovation and history. A philosophical critique]. *Quaderni, 91*, 47-59.

Ménissier, T. (2021). *Innovations : Une enquête philosophique [Innovations: A philosophical enquiry]*. Paris: Hermann.

Merleau-Ponty, M. (1985). *L'œil et l'esprit [The eye and the mind]*. Paris: Folio (1st ed. 1960).

Merleau-Ponty, M. (2013). *Phénoménologie de la perception [Phenomenology of perception]*. Nanterre: Gallimard (1st ed. 1945).

Michaud, Y. (2011). *L'art à l'état gazeux. Essai sur le triomphe de l'esthétique [Art in a gaseous state. Essay on the triumph of aesthetics]*. Domont: Pluriel (1st ed. 2003).

Miège, B. (1989). *La société conquise par la communication [Society conquered by communication]*. Grenoble: PUG.

Miège, B. (2004). *L'information - communication, objet de connaissance [Information – communication, object of knowledge]*. Brussels: De Boeck.

Miège, B. (2007). *La société conquise par la communication : Tome III Les Tic entre innovation technique et ancrage social [Society conquered by communication: Volume III ICT between technical innovation and social anchoring]*. Grenoble: Presses Universitaires de Grenoble.

Miège, B. (2015). *Contribution aux avancées de la connaissance en Information – Communication [Contribution to the advancement of knowledge in Information – Communication].* Bry-sur-Marne: INA Éditions.

Miège, B. (2017). *Les industries culturelles et créatives face à l'ordre de l'information et de la communication [Cultural and creative industries facing the information and communication order].* Grenoble: PUG.

Miège, B. (2020). *La numérisation en cours de la société. Points de repères et enjeux [The ongoing digitisation of society. Points de repères et enjeux].* Grenoble: PUG.

Miller, G. (2012). The Smartphone Psychology Manifesto. *Perspectives on Psychological Science, 7*(3), 221-237.

Moore, G. (2014). *Crossing the Chasm. Marketing and Selling Disruptive Products to Mainstream Customers.* NY: Harper Business Essential.

Mumford, L. (2000). *Art and Technics.* NY: Columbia University Press (1st ed. 1952).

Musso, P. (2003). *Critique des réseaux [Critique of networks].* Paris: PUF.

Niedenthal, P. (2007). Embodying Emotion. *Science, 316*, 1002-1005.

Nietzsche, F. (1967). *Werke in zwei Bänden. Band 2 [Works in two volumes. 2nd Vol.]* München: Carl Hanser.

Nietzsche, F. (1977). *Zur Genealogie der Moral. Eine Streitschrift [Genealogy of Morals. A polemical writing].* München: Wilhelm Goldmann Verlag (1st ed. 1887).

Nietzsche, F. (2006). *Jenseits von Gut und Böse [Beyond Good and Evil: Prelude to a Philosophy of the Future].* Köln: Anaconda (1st ed. 1886).

Nietzsche, F. (2008). *Götzendämmerung. Oder: Wie man mit dem Hammer philosophiert [Twilight of the Idols. Or: How to philosophise with a hammer].* Köln: Anaconda (1st ed. 1889).

Nietzsche, F. (2019). *Also sprach Zarathustra. Ein Buch für Alle und Keinen (8te Aufl.) [Thus Spoke Zarathustra. A book for everyone and no one (8th ed.)].* Hamburg: Nikol (1st ed. 1883).

Nobel, C. (2011, 02 14). *Clay Christensens's Milkshake Marketing* (Harvard Business School) Retrieved on 09 2020 from Working Knowledge.

Business Research for Business Leaders: https://hbswk.hbs.edu/item/clay-christensens-milkshake-marketing

Norman, D. (2004). *Emotional Design. Why I Love (or Hate) Everyday Things.* NY: Basic Books.

Norman, D. (2007). *The Design of Future Things.* NY: Basic Books.

Norman, D. (2013). *The Design of Everyday Things (Rev. Ed.).* Cambridge: MIT Press (1st ed. 1988).

Norman, D. & Verganti, R. (2013). Incremental and Radical Innovation: Design Research vs. Technology and Meaning Change. *Design Issues.* 30 (1). 78-96.

Offe, C. (2010). Was (falls überhaupt etwas) können wir uns heute unter politischem "Fortschritt" vorstellen? [What (if anything) can we imagine today by political 'progress'?] *WestEnd. Neue Zeitschrift für Sozialforschung, 2*, 3-14.

Petit, V. (2017). Perspectives sur le design. Métier, enseignement, recherche [Perspectives on design. Profession, teaching, research]. *Cahiers COSTECH, 1*, 31.

Picard, R. (1997). *Affective Computing.* London: MIT Press.

Plass, J., & Kaplan, U. (2016). Emotional Design in Digital Media for Learning. In S. Tettegah, & M. Gartmeier, *Emotions, Technology, Design, and Learning* (pp. 131-161). San Diego: Academic Press.

Poirson, M. (2014). Capitalisme artiste et optimisation du capital attentionnel [Artist capitalism and the optimization of attentional capital]. In Y. Citton (ed.), *L'économie de l'attention. Nouvel horizon du capitalisme ?* (pp. 267-286). Paris: La Découverte.

Polanyi, M. (2009). *The Tacit Dimension.* London: UCP (1st ed. 1966).

Quinton, P. (2002). *Les designs des images et des écritures. Pour une approche de la production graphique comme usage [The designs of images and writings. Pour une approche de la production graphique comme usage] (HDR).* Paris: Université Paris 7 Denis Diderot.

Rammert, W., Windeler, A., Knoblauch, H., & Hutter, M. (2018). *Innovation Society Today. Perspectives, Fields, and Cases.* Wiesbaden: Springer.

Redström, J. (2017). *Making Design Theory*. Cambridge: MIT Press.

Redwitz, G. (2010). *Die digital-vernetzte Wissensgesellschaft: Aufbruch ins 21. Jahrhundert [The digitally networked knowledge society: Start into the 21st century]*. München: Piper.

Reckwitz, A. (2019). *Die Erfindung der Kreativität. Zum Prozess gesellschaftlicher Ästhetisierung [The invention of creativity. On the process of social aestheticisation]*. Berlin: Suhrkamp.

Rimé, B. (2005). *Le partage social des émotions [The social sharing of emotions]*. Paris: PUF.

Ringel, M., Baeza, R., Grassl, F., Panandiker, R., & Harnoss, J. (2020). The Most Innovative Companies 2020. The Serial Innovation Imperative. *Boston Consulting Group*, 20.

Rogers, E. (1983). *Diffusion of Innovations (3rd ed.)*. NY: The Free Press (1st ed. 1962).

Rosa, H. (2005). *Beschleunigung. Die Veränderung der Zeitstrukturen in der Moderne [Acceleration. Change in the temporal structures of modern times]*. Frankfurt a.M.: Suhrkamp.

Rosa, H. (2013). *Beschleunigung und Entfremdung. Entwurf einer Kritischen Theorie spätmoderner Zeitlichkeit [Acceleration and Alienation. Draft of a Critical Theory of Modern Temporality]*. Frankfurt a.M.: Suhrkamp.

Rosa, H. (2015a). Capitalism as a Spiral of Dynamisation: Sociology as Social Critique. In K. Dörre, S. Lessenich, & H. Rosa, *Sociology, Capitalism, Critique* (pp. 67-97). London: Suhrkamp.

Rosa, H. (2015b). Escalation: The Crisis of Dynamic Stabilisation and the Prospect of Resonance. In K. Dörre, S. Lessenich, & H. Rosa, *Sociology, Capitalism, Critique* (pp. 280-305). London: Verso.

Rosa, H. (2016). *Resonanz. Eine Soziologie der Weltbeziehungen [Resonance. A sociology of global relations]*. Berlin: Suhrkamp.

Rosa, H. (2018). *Unverfügbarkeit [Unavailability]*. Wien: Residenz.

Roth, E. F., Koivuniemi, A., & Doherty, R. (2020, 10 29). *Growth & Innovation*. Retrieved from McKinsey & Company: https://www.mckinsey.com/business-functions/strategy-and-corporate-finance/how-we-help-clients/growth-and-innovation

Sagioglou, C., & Greitemeyer, T. (2014). Facebook's emotional consequences: Why Facebook causes a decrease in mood and why people still use it. *Computers in Human Behavior, 35*, 359-363.

Schachter, S. (1964). The interaction of cognitive and physiological determinants of emotional state. In Berkowitz, L. (Ed.), *Advances in experimental social psychology* (Vol. 1). NY: Academic Press.

Scherer, K. (1998). Emotionsprozesse im Medienkontext [Emotional processes in the media context]. *Medienpsychology, 10 (4)*, 277-293.

Scherer, K. (2005). What are emotions? And how can they be measured? [*Social Science Information, 44 (4)*, 695-729.

Schumpeter, J. (2008). *Capitalism, Socialism and Democracy.* NY: Harper (1st ed. 1942).

Simon, H. (1971). Designing Organizations for an Information-Rich World. In M. Greenberger, *Computers, communications, and the public interest* (pp. 37-72). Baltimore: The Johns Hopkins Press.

Simondon, G. (2012). *Du mode d'existence des objets technique [On the mode of existence of technical objects].* Paris: Aubier (1st ed. 1958).

Staii, A. (2014). Attention ou trafic? Critiques de quelques illusions d'économies [Attention or traffic? Critiques of some illusions of savings]. In Y. Citton, *L'économie de l'attention. Nouvel horizon du capitalisme ? [The economy of attention. Nouvel horizon du capitalisme?]* (pp. 136-146). Paris: La Découverte.

Stevens, G., & Burley, J. (1997). 3000 raw ideas equal 1 commercial success! *Research Technology Management, 40*(3), 18.

Tan, S. (2000). Emotion, Art and the Humanities. In M. Lewis, & J. Haviland-Jones, *Handbook of Emotions 2nd ed.* (pp. 116-131). New York, NY: Guilford Publications.

Taylor, M., & Botan, C. (2004). Public Relations: State of the Field. *Journal of Communication*, 54(4), 645-661.

Tcherkassof, A. (2008). *Les émotions et leurs expressions [Emotions and their expressions].* Grenoble: PUG.

Trentmann, F. (2016). *Empire of Things. How I Became a World of Consumers, from the Fifteenth Century to the Twenty-first. How I Became a World of*

Consumers, from the Fifteenth Century to the Twenty-first century]. London: Penguin Books.

UMI (2020, 08 26). *UMI (United Motion Ideas).* Retrieved from https://www.umi.us/fr/

Varela, F., Thompson, E., & Rosch, E. (2016). *The Embodied Mind. Cognitive Science and Human Experience (Rev. Ed.).* Cambridge: MIT Press (1st ed. 1991).

Vial, S. (2020). *Le design [The design].* Paris: PUF (1st ed. 2015).

Virilio, P. (1990). *L'inertie populaire [Popular inertia].* Paris: Christian Bourgouis Editor.

Vorderer, p. (2015). Der mediatisierte Lebenswandel: Permanently online, permanently connected [The mediatised way of life: Permanently online, permanently connected]. *Springer Fachmedien, 60*, 259-276.

Vorderer, P., Kroemer, N., & Schneider, F. M. (2016). Permanently online - Permanently connected: Explorations into university students' use of social media and mobile smart devices. *Computers in Human Behavior, 63*(63), 694-703.

Walter, A. (2019). *Emotional Design.* Paris: Groupe Eyrolles.

Weber, M. (2002). *The Protestant Ethic and the "Spirit" of Capitalism.* NY: Penguin (1st ed. 1905).

Weller, T. (2007). Information history: its importance, relevance and future. *Aslib Proceedings, 59*(4/5), 437-448.

Wiggershaus, R. (1991). *Die Frankfurter Schule. Geschichte. Theoretische Entwicklung. Politische Bedeutung [The Frankfurt School. History. Theoretical development. Political significance].* München: dtv (1st ed. 1988).

Zacklad, M. (2017). Design, conception, création. Vers une théorie interdisciplinaire du Design [Design, conception, creation. Towards an interdisciplinary theory of Design]. p. 22. Retrieved from https://www.academia.edu/35516081/Design_conception_création_vers_u ne_théorie_interdisciplinaire_du_Design

Zacklad, Manuel. (2019). Le design de l'information : textualisation, documentarisation, auctorialisation [Information design: textualisation, documentarisation, auctorialisation]. *Communication & languages.* N° 199 (37). 10.3917/comla1.199.0037.

Glossary

Critical Design = Introduced by Dunne (2006) and popularized by Dunne & Raby (2013), the term describes critical approaches to Design. Critical Design's vocation is to question societal practices and norms. Dunne & Raby (2013) define it as follows: *"Critical Design is critical thinking translated into materiality"* (p. 35).[35] It can include the highlighting of ambiguous and/or negative affects. I will refer to this approach as an example of a design practice that takes a normative stance by questioning ideologies and beliefs. The notion implies a skeptical attitude, for the designer, towards societal norms. A widespread synonym is *Speculative Design.*

Design = The English term means both design (which can be engineering) and creation. I refer to this term in the sense of creation. Design is an expression of the creative forces of a human being. It represents the intention to manifest itself to the world and mainly to manipulate it *for the better.* Design is thus conditioned by ideological assumptions. The process of design becomes more complex during modernity by including a multiplicity of involved professions (Miège, 2017). In saturated markets, design represents the potential for added value, and thus competitive advantage. The practice of design involves certain intellectual acrobatics to reconcile utopian imagination with the constraints of reality – according to the industrial necessities of the given project. For a precise definition of different design types, see the three-dimensional definition of Zacklad (2017, p. 5) presented in figure 4.

Innovation = The *guru* of innovation – Everett Rogers – originally defined an innovation as follows:

> "An *innovation* is an idea, practice, or object that is perceived as new by an individual or other unit of adoption. It matters little, so far as human behavior is concerned, whether or not an idea is 'objectively' new as measured by the lapse of time since its first

---

[35] Our translation. Original text: "Critical design is critical thought translated into materiality." (Dunne & Raby, 2013, p. 35).

use or discovery. The perceived newness of the idea for the individual determines his or her reaction to it. If the idea seems new to the individual, it is an innovation." (Rogers, 1983/1962, p. 11).

The important point of this definition is that an innovation is subjective. Rogers characterizes the diffusion of an innovation according to its relative advantage (if the advantage is perceived to be superior, diffusion will be faster), compatibility (between the innovation and existing know-how, practices and values), complexity (is the innovation difficult to understand?), testability (is the innovation testable on a limited basis?) and observability (to what degree are the effects of the innovation visible to others?). These five characteristics condition the speed of diffusion and market penetration (see Figure 6). Innovation includes political, social, or ecological ones, and permeates all spheres of society. The innovation sector has become a key force in modern economies (Rammert et al., 2018, p. 3). Nowadays, innovation is an obligation for socioeconomic actors to remain competitive.

User Centered Turn = Refers to a change in perspective on the development of products and services at the end of the 20th Century, which is becoming less technocentric and more focused on the user. The *User Centered Turn* is responsible for the consideration of affects in the development of innovations, as well as for the emergence of *emotional design* (Walter, 2019; Norman, 2004).

Psycho-somatic-affective competencies = I propose the term *psycho-somatic-affective* to indicate the intertwining of mind, cognition, affect, and the human body. It represents a holistic approach to anthropology, following Embodiment (Niedenthal, 2007), resembling the concept of *Enactivism* from Varela, Thompson & Rosch (2016/1991), or the *affective body* by Martin-Juchat (2008a; 2008b), following the phenomenology of Heidegger (1963/1927) and Merleau-Ponty (2013/1945). When talking about the psychic, somatic or affective dimension, then, I use the term *psycho-somatic-affective* to indicate that a phenomena in one of these dimensions automatically effects the others. The term is opposed to the Cartesian dualism of René Descartes. In this book I conceptualize design practices as psycho-somatic-affective competencies.

Semiotic concretization = The task of the designer is, among other things, the semiotic translation of a given content from the specificities of one medium into another. For example, in the case of usage scenarios, the designer translates an innovation concept from literary descriptions into images. This process requires thinking about the content through the specificities of a given medium, which is a form of semiotic translation. Thereby, the content becomes more concrete. It resembles Adorno's definition of form as "sedimented content" (1992/1973, p. 15).

Dialectic of reason = Theoretical concept established by the Frankfurt School and presented in Horkheimer & Adorno's *Dialektik der Aufklärung* ("The Dialectic of Reason") (2013/1947), it refers to the ambivalence inherent in emancipation through rationality. The growth of a strictly rational relationship to reality leads to a decrease in archaic, animalistic, spiritual, bodily knowledge. The approach leads to Adorno's (1975/1966) negative dialectic, according to whom modern progress represents a degradation. For example, Auschwitz is taken as a metaphysical fact revealing human Nature, representing the barbaric side of modern progress.

Modernity = Term corresponding to the contemporary era. The determination of its beginning and its characteristics varies greatly. Some historians propose to place the beginning of modernity around the 15th Century (Weller, 2007; José Ortega y Gasset, 1952/1942, p. 14). Sometimes its beginnings are observed during the mid to late 20th Century, but more often it is associated with the era of industrialization, i.e. from the end of the 18th Century and then in the course of the 19th Century, until the 20th Century. The middle and end of the 20th Century are rather associated with the emergence of information, knowledge and communication societies, and finally the connected society (Miège, 1989; 2004; 2007; Redwitz, 2010; Rammert et al., 2018). Their common aspects are societal phenomena related to the emergence of ICT. According to Rosa (2015a), modernity is marked by the obligation to innovate and by exponential growth, which explains the importance of design practices and innovation projects. According to Rosa (2015a; 2015b), modern societies fall into crisis if they fail to innovate. He calls this the need for "dynamic stabilization". Capitalism is identified as a key force influencing modernity (Doerre, Lessenich & Rosa, 2015). Modernity can be closely linked with globalization and connectivity. Giddens (1995) characterizes modernity by a division of space-time and functional differentiations through techno-scientific rationality. I understand modernity according to Rosa (2005; 2013; 2015a; 2015b; 2016; 2018). When I refer to *modernity*, I refer to the dynamics initiated by the scientific revolution of the 15th and 16th Centuries, but more specifically to the second half of the 20th Century, which was marked by the emergence of contemporary ICTs, and, even more specifically, to the innovative developments of the early 21th Century. When I speak of contemporary ICTs, I refer to the info-communicational structures as they have been identified since the beginning of the 21st Century, particularly since the first iPhone was launched in 2007.

Technoscientific rationality = I use the term following Habermas (1973/1968), referring to functionalist, positivist and post-positivist thinking (Gavard-Perret et al., 2018) dominant in modern industrialized societies. Technoscientific rationality represents, according to Habermas (1973/1968; 1974), a totalitarian ideology, which should be criticized because of its tendency to present itself as the *only and true knowledge* (Habermas, 1974). According to Habermas (1974) and Marcuse (1991/1964), it serves to justify modern power structures. The dialectic of reason (Horkheimer & Adorno, 2013/1947), describes the ambiguities and ambivalences of technoscientific rationality.